JULIUS CAESAR'S INVASION OF BRITAIN

SOLVING A 2,000-YEAR-OLD MYSTERY

To Pam

With best wishes

Roger Nolan

For Joseph and Charles

JULIUS CAESAR'S INVASION OF BRITAIN

SOLVING A 2,000-YEAR-OLD MYSTERY

ROGER NOLAN

FRONTLINE
BOOKS

JULIUS CAESAR'S INVASION OF BRITAIN
Solving a 2,000-Year-Old Mystery

First published in Great Britain in 2018 by Frontline Books,
an imprint of Pen & Sword Books Ltd, Yorkshire - Philadelphia

Typeset in India by Vman Infotech Private Limited
Printed and bound by TJ International

Pen & Sword Books Ltd incorporates the imprints of Pen & Sword Archaeology,
Air World Books, Atlas, Aviation, Battleground, Discovery, Family History, History,
Maritime, Military, Naval, Politics, Social History, Transport, True Crime, Claymore
Press, Frontline Books, Praetorian Press, Seaforth Publishing and White Owl

For a complete list of Pen & Sword titles please contact:

PEN & SWORD BOOKS LTD
47 Church Street, Barnsley, South Yorkshire, S70 2AS, UK.
E-mail: enquiries@pen-and-sword.co.uk
Website: www.pen-and-sword.co.uk

Or

PEN AND SWORD BOOKS,
1950 Lawrence Road, Havertown, PA 19083, USA
E-mail: Uspen-and-sword@casematepublishers.com
Website: www.penandswordbooks.com

Contents

Acknowledgements

My initial thanks go to Peter Salway whose footnote in his excellent book *Roman Britain* was the catalyst which started me on the investigation which resulted in the discovery of the marching camps established by Julius Caesar's army.

Although this book has by and large been a one-man exercise, I have had help from a number of people and organisations during the long period of research and investigation.

In the early days of my researches, I had much help from the staff at the museum at Canterbury.

In particular, I owe a debt of gratitude to Jak Showell for his kind advice and wise counsel based on his vast experience of authorship and the means of bringing a book to publication as well as his encouragement during the writing of this book.

Many thanks to Kevin Diver of Thurrock Council for opening the Coalhouse Fort at East Tilbury to enable me to photograph the Thames crossing from the ramparts of the fort.

My grateful thanks are due to John Grehan at Frontline Books for guiding me through the complicated process of commissioning this book.

Finally, very special thanks to Sally Robinson who first suggested I set down in writing the results of my researches over the years and supported me and encouraged me throughout the process of writing this book.

Roger Nolan,
Littlestone-on-Sea,
2018.

Foreword

The great fascination of the early history of the British Isles is not what we know, but what we don't know, for this opens up the opportunity for discovery. Such discoveries add to our growing knowledge and understanding of the past, though some sow confusion when they appear to counter previously-accepted theories. This is no more so than with the invasions of Julius Caesar in the first century BC. With seemingly little archaeological evidence to guide us, the landing places and routes through southern England taken by Caesar's army have been determined more through calculated interpretation than hard facts. That was until the uncovering in 2017 of a massive Roman encampment at Pegwell Bay on the Isle of Thanet.

As is often the case, this discovery was made during archaeological excavations before a new construction programme, in this instance, the building of the new East Kent Access road. The site, which may be up to twenty hectares in size, includes a defensive ditch some four to five metres deep and two metres wide, has yielded finds that have been identified as first century BC, including a Roman pilum (javelin). It has been said by archaeologists from the University of Leicester headed by Dr Andrew Fitzpatrick, that the shape of the ditch at Pegwell Bay is very similar to some of the Roman defences at Alésia in France, where a decisive battle in the Gallic Wars took place in 52 BC.

There is, therefore, a high probability that this is one, and arguably the most important, of Caesar's camps. As has been stated by the spokesperson for the University of Leicester dig, the Isle of Thanet had not previously been considered a likely landing place because it was separated from the mainland by the Wantsum Channel and this still presents us with a problem reconciling Pegwell Bay with Julius Caesar's own detailed account of his invasion of Britain.

Looking at Caesar's first invasion in 55 BC, we read that 'he advanced about seven miles … and stationed his fleet over against an open and level shore. But the barbarians, upon perceiving the design of the Romans, sent forward their cavalry and charioteers, a class of warriors of whom it is their practice to make great use in their battles, and following with the rest of their forces, endeavoured to prevent our men landing.' The question must be asked, how did the Britons move along the coast and then transport their horses and chariots across the Wantsum Channel in time to oppose Caesar's soldiers before they had waded ashore. Movement along land, following simple tracks, was notoriously slow compared with sea travel, which is why, as Caesar states, the Britons sent forward their cavalry and charioteers as these were the only ones that could keep pace with the Roman fleet.

The Britons could not have known where Caesar would make landfall, which is why they 'followed' the invasion fleet. When it was seen that the Romans were going to attempt a landing on the Isle of Thanet, they would, somehow, have had to manhandle their chariots, along with what must have been a considerable number of horses, onto boats to cross the Wantsum Channel in time to be ahead of the Romans – if indeed they had a large number of suitably large vessels waiting for them to jump into. None of this could have happened.

Furthermore, there would have been no advantage to the Romans in landing on the Isle of Thanet, as they still had water to cross to reach the mainland. Some indication of the degree of obstacle the Wantsum Channel represented can be gleaned from the investigations of the Kent Archaeological Society paper presented by F. W. Hardman and W. P. D. Stebbing: 'We conceive it as a natural arc-shaped stream of tidal water cutting off Thanet from the mainland with a breadth of about two miles and a depth of about forty feet and with wide open ends. It formed a safe roadstead for ships and a sheltered line of communication with the Thames.'[1] Likewise, T. Rice Holmes declared unequivocally, that: 'Thanet, as everyone knows, was an island in Caesar's time'[2], and as far back as Bede who wrote in the early eighth century that, 'On the east of Kent is the large Isle of Thanet containing according to the English way of reckoning, 600 families, divided from the other land by the river Wantsum, which is about three furlongs over.'[3]

Equally, one would imagine, that the British would have waited on the mainland for the invaders to cross the Wantsum Channel before attacking, as this would have given them more time to bring up their foot warriors.

Lastly, as Roger Nolan has found, none of this ties in with Caesar's account, which is in other regards, quite specific in its details.

Having landed and defeated the British (who had agreed to submit to Caesar) we learn many of the Roman ships were damaged by a high spring tide and a severe storm. The British decided to take advantage of this and renewed hostilities, by attacking a legion which had been sent out to forage. The legion was taken by surprise and almost overwhelmed. The Romans were very astute campaigners and it is hard to imagine that, while not expecting to be attacked by the Britons, they had not had sentries watching the Wantsum Channel. Indeed, according to Caesar, the approach of the enemy was detected by the dust they raised as they marched. Nothing about this account indicates in any way that the Roman camp was on the Isle of Thanet.

So we can safely discount Pegwell Bay as the landing place of the Julian invasion of 55 BC. But what of Caesar's much larger expedition of the following year?

On this second occasion, Caesar wrote that he ordered all the ships 'to assemble at Portus Itius, from which port he had learned that the passage into Britain was shortest, [being only] about thirty miles from the continent'. Pegwell Bay is much further from Continental Europe than thirty miles, so, clearly, Caesar had no intention of heading for anywhere near the Isle of Thanet.

Of the expedition, Caesar then wrote: 'in consequence of the wind dying away about midnight, and being carried on too far by the tide, when the sun rose, espied Britain passed on his left. Then, again, following the change of tide, he urged on with the oars that he might make that part of the island which he had discovered the preceding summer had the best landing place or places.

From this we can see that Caesar had travelled too far north from his intended landing place, because the land was on his left and that when the tide turned he urged his men to row hard back to a place he had identified in 55 BC as being an ideal landing ground. There is not much land to be seen on the east-facing coast beyond Pegwell Bay before the coastline turns north, and the short distance to be covered from even its furthest extremity, North Foreland, to Pegwell Bay would hardly require the great effort from his men that Caesar comments on. We should look further south for the ideal landing place of the 54 BC expedition.

After landing, Caesar left his ships 'fastened at anchor upon an even and open shore'. While such a description may seem quite clear, as Birgitta Hoffmann has pointed out, we might be taking Caesar's words too literally. An even and open shore *'plano et aperto'* described by Caesar as the place of the 55 BC landing, could simply mean one that was free of rocks or one that was a wide beach location, as *aperto* means open in every interpretation of that word.

Equally, *'mollis et aperto'* Caesar's description of the 54 BC site as 'soft and open', could also be interpreted differently, in that *mollis* can mean soft but can also mean gentle and pleasant. In this context, Hoffmann observes, Caesar might simply be stating that the place where he landed was an ideal beach location. Hoffman concludes that it is impossible, therefore, to identify the exact locations of the Julian landings based solely on Caesar's account.[4]

Nevertheless, having landed, Caesar then marched inland to defeat the British once and for all. The route Caesar took, and the major battle he fought with the British, is the main subject of Roger Nolan's discoveries which are detailed in this book.

Shortly after the battle, as the Romans were about to pursue the defeated enemy, Caesar received news that, 'a very great storm having arisen, almost all the ships were dashed to pieces and cast upon the shore, because neither the anchors and cables could resist, nor could the sailors and pilots sustain the violence of the storm; and thus great damage was received by that collision of the ships'.

Quite why Caesar hadn't learnt from his previous experience, and beached his ships, remains a mystery. Nevertheless, he rode back to the coast to see the extent of the damage, which was considerable. He then ordered the ships to be pulled up onto the shore and a large fortification built which would accommodate both his troops and the ships. For that, no better place could be found than Pegwell Bay. Remembering that the British had attacked his camp the previous year and that the bulk of his army had marched inland, relocating to the Isle of Thanet gave the troops left on the coast a far better chance of protecting themselves with the Wantsum Channel acting as a moat. It is quite conceivable that this is the camp which has recently been discovered. Roger puts forward an alternative proposal.

I turn next to the main thrust of Roger Nolan's work, the discovery of Caesar's temporary marching camps. Without anticipating Roger's revelations, it is a fact that, until now, no one had found any evidence of Caesar's camps, which is unusual as so many Roman temporary marching camps – around 150 – have been found in England alone, and none of those are in Kent.[5] These discoveries are key to unravelling both the site of the first major land battle in British history – that which until now had been thought to have been at Bigbury Camp – and the place where Caesar crossed the Thames, usually assumed to have been at Brentford. Roger quite convincingly dismisses both locations, and his work would be significant for these two conclusions alone. But there is more. The temporary marching camps, the site of the battle with the Britons, the location of the ford on the Thames, all contribute to Roger Nolan's identification of the probable place where Caesar landed in 54 BC.

John Grehan,
Shoreham-by-Sea,
May 2018.

List of Illustrations

1 The coast of Britain on a clear day which is the view Caesar would no doubt have seen when planning his expedition.

2 This plaque is on the beach between Walmer and Deal and it asserts Walmer's claim to be the landing place for the first invasion in 55 BC.

3 Dover from the sea. This is where Caesar rode at anchor after having seen the enemy lined up on the cliffs in 55 BC. It is also the probable site of the landing the following year.

4 The defensive ditch on the western side of the camp at Denge Wood overlooking the River Stour.

5 The defensive ditch on the eastern side of the camp at Denge Wood, looking towards Chartham Downs and Iffin Wood.

6 The Long Barrow known as Julliberrie's Grave where tradition had it that one of Caesar's military tribunes, Quintus Laberius Durus, was buried.

7 A view of Chartham Downs from Iffin Wood. As Caesar wrote, the enemy took up a position on the hills at a distance from the camp and then suddenly swooped down on the legionaries from all sides.

8 Another view of Chartham Downs showing the steepness of the land on the northern side of the valley where the Romans were out foraging and where the battle was fought.

9 The Roman fort at Kemsley. The massive ramparts and the ditch are to some extent obscured by the considerable undergrowth and also possibly may have been enhanced by the construction of Swale Way which runs alongside.

10 Much of the Kemsley fort has been lost to commercial use. In particular, a large electricity substation covers much of the site. This view shows part of the ramparts within the electricity substation site.

11 This is where Caesar crossed the Thames, photographed from the ramparts of the Coalhouse Fort at East Tilbury. In Roman times, there had been a ford here and later, when that had become unusable, it became a ferry crossing.

12 Sadly, nothing now remains of the Roman Camp at East Tilbury as the site has been turned over to gravel extraction. However, the area was extensively excavated in the late 1960s and early 1970s which was known as the Mucking Archaeological Excavation.

13 These ramparts are at Loughton Camp in Epping Forest. Loughton Camp was Caesar's last marching camp before the storming of the Catuvellaunian camp at Wheathampstead.

14 The rampart and ditch at Loughton Camp.

15 The ramparts and ditch at Devil's Dyke which is the local name for the fortifications at the Catuvellaunian camp at Wheathampstead.

16 A sign at the entrance to Devils Dyke at Wheathampstead.

List of Maps

Introduction

It all started with an observation in a footnote to a book I was reading some years ago. Having had a lifelong interest in the Roman occupation of Britain, I had decided to read Peter Salway's excellent book *Roman Britain* published by the Oxford University Press.

In the footnote, the author expresses surprise that none of Caesar's temporary camps inland had been found unlike the large numbers known from later Roman campaigns.[1]

This struck me as very odd. I was familiar with many of the Roman temporary marching camps in Britain especially those north of Hadrian's Wall and had taken the opportunity to visit as many as possible when I found myself in the north. By their very definition, temporary camps would have been constructed in a short period and then occupied for an equally short time. Yet, why would those from the Claudian invasion of 43 AD onwards still be visible whilst temporary camps from less than 100 years earlier seem no longer to exist?

I realised that any investigation to find the temporary camps would be helped by the fact that Caesar himself wrote a detailed account of his two invasions in 55 BC and 54 BC in his book on the Gallic Wars[2] and that that detailed account must surely contain information to enable investigations into his travels in Kent and beyond.

So, I got the bit between my teeth and living in Kent as I do and knowing that Caesar had passed through Kent, I decided I would set about trying to find whether or not there was any evidence for his invasions still to be seen.

What started to emerge, finally resulted in a fascinating detective story which would eventually lead to a discovery of all the aspects of Caesar's campaigns in Britain, especially in 54 BC and enable a full analysis of the campaigns, explain the reasons why Caesar undertook them and an assessment of their success when set against other similar historical campaigns in Britain.

After all, this was one of history's greatest generals and he had set foot in southeast England. How marvellous it would be to find evidence of his presence here.

Another interest since I was young has been a love of maps and I could spend ages poring over them just to find anything of interest.

So, the first thing I did after deciding that I would have a go at solving the Caesar mystery was to examine closely a detailed map of Kent. Almost immediately, I spotted the tell-tale outline of a Roman marching camp. The investigation had begun.

The two invasions of Julius Caesar, one of the most famous if not the most famous Roman of them all, have consistently failed to be investigated satisfactorily, despite the fact that, uniquely, Caesar himself wrote a detailed account of the invasions in his master work, *De Bello Gallico* – The Gallic Wars.

The Romans invaded Britain in 55 BC and 54 BC under Julius Caesar and again in 43 AD under the Emperor Claudius. The landings of Julius Caesar in Britain are not often discussed, mainly because they tend to be regarded as invasions which were primarily failures. It is generally considered that the only successful invasion was that of Claudius in 43 AD which brought about the beginning of the permanent occupation of Britain by the Romans.

However, this view is somewhat simplistic and does not fit in with the reputation of Caesar as one of the great generals of the ancient world. Caesar would have been unlikely to make mistakes and therefore would he have done so in Britain?

The occupation of the islands following the Claudian Invasion has left much evidence on the landscape of Britain, not least, the numerous marching camps and as already mentioned, many of these are to be found in northern England and Scotland.

It has always been a puzzle as to why no-one had ever found any tangible evidence of the invasions of Caesar in 55 and 54 BC in the south of England and in particular no evidence of his marching camps. Surely there must have been such camps? Such a large army would have left its mark on the countryside. It is possible that the earthworks built to shelter the fleet on land may have been discovered as a result of the recent archaeological excavations at Pegwell Bay in north Kent. These excavations are discussed in greater detail later in the book. However, they have not yielded any information on the passage of Caesar's army through the south of England and in particular the site of any marching camps.

I suspect that many will explain this lack of concrete evidence by the fact that Caesar's invasions lasted only two years but the Claudian invasions resulted in Roman occupation for the next 400 years.

However, there is another possible explanation for the lack of evidence and that is that perhaps we have all been looking in the wrong places.

Attempts had been made in the past to discover and identify the details of Caesars invasions, most notably the work of T. Rice Holmes, an amateur antiquarian, in the late nineteenth and early twentieth century and before him, the French Emperor Napoleon III in the mid nineteenth century as well as a number of other antiquarians before them. Many different theories were propounded by the various authors, most of them differing from each other and none of them giving any proof.

The nineteenth century saw the heyday of researches into Caesar's invasions of Britain and this period of intense research by very many historians and antiquarians culminated in the publication in 1907 of a book entitled *Ancient Britain and the Invasions of Julius Caesar* by Rice Holmes.

Rice Holme's book is comprehensive and very detailed and in it he carefully analyses many of the earlier theories and draws conclusions based on his own research. As a result, he sets out his theories as to the landings and the progress through southern England. However, his conclusions are not always entirely logically-based and are open to question. Nevertheless, these are the theories we are all familiar with today.[3]

Rice Holmes concluded that in 54 BC Julius Caesar landed near Deal, proceeded to Bigbury camp west of modern Canterbury where he fought a battle with the Ancient Britons, then proceeded to Brentford where he crossed the Thames, doubled back north of the Thames and met up with the Trinovantes, a tribe based in what is now East Essex who were allies of the Romans at that time. Lastly Caesar then proceeded to what is modern Wheathampstead in Hertfordshire where he sacked Cassivellaunus' camp. Ever since Rice Holmes' book was published in 1907, the academic world has tended to accept his theories as fact and little further work seems to have been undertaken on the subject.

The general consensus seems to be that all questions have been answered, we know the site of the landings and the route of the invasions and therefore very little additional research has been or has needed to be carried out. Indeed, most modern accounts of Caesar's invasions reproduce Rice Holmes' theories verbatim as if they were fact.

The modern world is so very different compared with the late nineteenth century, when Rice Holmes was carrying out his research and writing his book. We have a degree of mobility unheard of prior to 1907 where cars can now take us wherever we wish to go to carry out field work. Modern maps are far more sophisticated than those available in the nineteenth century. We have the internet which gives us access to sophisticated enhanced satellite topography as well as online access to the greatest source of information way beyond anything available in the past.

It is this modern environment that really demands that we revisit the past theories relating to the invasions. It is appropriate that we should use all of these modern facilities to have another look at the question of where Julius Caesar travelled through Southern Britain and look for any remaining evidence of his invasion army.

One of the most significant facilities available in the modern age is access through the medium of the internet to almost all of the previous studies carried out in the past. This, together with the fact that we have Caesar's own account in his book on the Gallic Wars, should take us as near as can be possible to finding out the truth and answering the various questions.

Of course, whatever conclusions we reach as to the evidence of Caesar's landings and progress through southern England, we can never provide definitive proof. However, circumstantial evidence when combined into an overall picture of the landing and transit through Britain can, in the right circumstances, bring us close to the realisation that the issue has been solved short of an actual proof.

This book provides that evidence.

Chapter One

Caesar's own account[1]

C aesar had conquered most of Gaul by 55 BC, but he decided to undertake an expedition to Britain because he was aware that during his Gallic campaigns, the Gauls had received regular reinforcements from the Britons. He was interested to see what the island and its inhabitants were like, find where their harbours were and in particular discover the best places to land an army. However, it was late summer, and he would not be able to stay long before winter would set in.

Although there was a significant amount of trade between the Gauls and the Britons, and Caesar quizzed as many traders as he could, he was unable to find where there were harbours sufficient to accommodate a large fleet of ships. Clearly at this stage he was thinking of the possibility of a large invasion rather than a mere expedition.

He decided that the best thing to do would be to send someone to reconnoitre the coast and he chose one of his officers, Volusenus, who was despatched to make a reconnaissance and return as soon as possible.

Caesar then marched his army into the territory of the Morini, which stretched from south of what is modern Calais to roughly modern Ostend because he states that from this territory, was the shortest crossing to Britain.

When the Britons got wind of what Caesar was planning, they sent envoys who offered hostages and undertook not to interfere with Caesar's plans. Caesar sent one of his trusted associates, Commius, to act as his ambassador in discussions with the various British tribes. He had recently installed Commius as the king of a northern Gallic tribe called the Atrebates and he knew Commius was respected by the Britons.

Caesar sent Commius back to Britain with the representatives of the British tribes and told him to tell the Britons the Romans were coming and that they could be assured they would be under the protection of Rome. Meanwhile, Volusenus returned after four days and reported to Caesar on what he had found.

Just before Caesar was about to leave, a delegation from the local tribe, the Morini, came to apologise for previous hostile action and to assure Caesar that they would obey his commands in future. Not exactly taking them at their word, Caesar took a large number of hostages from the tribe to ensure their newly-declared compliance.

Caesar assembled eighty transports, sufficient to carry two legions, and some warships to carry the officers. In addition, eighteen transports were assembled some eight miles along the coast, to carry the cavalry.

Two generals, Sabinus and Cotta, were left behind with the rest of the army with orders to march against another tribe, the Menapii, and the remainder of the Morini who had not promised to obey Caesar. A third general, Publius Sulpicius Rufus, was left to hold the embarkation harbour.

The weather was good, and Caesar set sail around midnight. The cavalry were sent to a port eight miles away, but they were delayed, failed to rendezvous with the rest of the invasion fleet and were forced to land back on the continent.

When Caesar reached the coast of Britain, he found that the enemy had duped him, despite their earlier undertakings, and were lined up on the cliffs above the shore. Realising that the army would be sitting ducks because the Britons could hurl javelins at them onto the narrow beaches under the cliffs, he decided that he should not land there and rode at anchor out to sea for six hours while he considered his options.

He held a conference with his generals and senior officers, emphasising that instant obeying of orders would be necessary as things happen so quickly in battle. He then found that the wind and tide had changed so he sailed about seven miles further on and ran the ships on an evenly sloping beach free from obstacles.

2

The Britons advanced into the water to oppose the landing of the invaders, but the Romans found that their ships grounded a fair way out to sea because of the gently sloping beach. The troops had to jump in the water weighed down with their armour and weapons. This was something Roman troops were unused to. As a result, Caesar ordered the warships to row hard and to beach nearer the shore line, where they were able to assault the Britons with slings, bows and artillery. Even then, the troops were reluctant to disembark and one brave man, who was the bearer of the eagle of the 10th Legion, jumped into the water (later commentators say he jumped onto a nearby rock) and shouted to his comrades that unless they jumped, they might lose their eagle which would have been shameful for any legion.

This prompted most of the other troops to jump into the water and as a result the army was able to engage with the enemy.

The battle that ensued was touch and go but eventually, the Roman troops took the beach and chased the enemy off, although they couldn't pursue them because the Roman cavalry had not arrived.

The Britons then sued for peace and although they had attacked the Romans having earlier said they would not, nevertheless and surprisingly, Caesar forgave them but did insist on further hostages to ensure that the peace would hold.

The cavalry eventually sailed from its northern port four days later but when they were close to the British coast, they were hit by a violent storm, some being swept back to their home port and others driven westward to the south of the island. In view of this disaster, the cavalry transports all returned to the continent.

The storm was clearly severe and the ships which had brought the infantry, and which had been beached on the English coast, were also waterlogged and some were destroyed. The situation was critical as the troops had no reserves of food and would have to return to the continent before winter.

The Britons got to hear of this predicament and decided it would be a good idea to take advantage of the situation and attack the Romans at their camp on the coast. At first Caesar was unaware that the locals were about to renew hostilities but came to realise something was afoot when further hostages he had been promised failed to materialise.

He sent foraging parties out to gather corn from the local fields and set about repairing the damaged ships. All but twelve were repaired.

While the repairs to the ships were underway, the guards at the gates of the camp noticed clouds of dust in the distance. Caesar knew immediately what this meant and hurried off with those soldiers who had been on guard duty and found that the enemy were engaging the men of the 7th Legion who were out cutting corn. The enemy had surrounded the legion with cavalry and chariots. The British were adept at using chariots and were even able to control them on steep hills.

The Romans found the enemy's tactics unnerving and Caesar decided that the safest option would be to lead the legion back to the camp. He then drew up his forces in battle formation in front of the camp and overpowered the enemy. He chased after them, killing many and, as a reprisal, set fire to as many buildings as he could find in the surrounding countryside.

Once again, envoys came to sue for peace and once again Caesar demanded hostages but twice as many this time as before.

However, Caesar decided that enough was enough. The autumn equinox was imminent with the consequential deterioration in the weather. He had achieved his aims of being the first Roman to lead an expedition to Britain and he had subdued the local tribes. It was time to get back to Gaul, and with his repaired ships, he sailed back to the continent.

Caesar must have learnt much from his expedition. One thing in particular he had found, was that the British could not be trusted. They would surrender when beaten but with no intention of continuing to act peaceably, especially if an opportunity arose to attack the Romans.

Caesar returned from his first invasion clearly angry at the duplicity of the British tribes and almost certainly he had already decided that he would undertake another invasion the following year.

After returning from Britain, Caesar went to spend the winter in Italy, but he left his generals with the task of modifying all the ships in the fleet to enable heavier cargoes to be carried, lowering the freeboard to facilitate easier loading and unloading, and also to build a considerable number of new ships. All ships were to be converted so as to be able to be rowed as well as sailed.[2]

Caesar makes it clear that whereas the invasion in 55 BC was a skirmish, this new expedition was going to be a full-blown invasion.

When Caesar got back from Italy, he was delighted to find that his men had built and equipped six hundred cargo ships and twenty-eight warships. Not only that, but the ships would be ready for launching within a few days.

Caesar ordered all the ships to assemble at Portus Itius while, meanwhile, he took four legions and eight hundred cavalry to put down an internecine civil war within the tribe of the Treveri who inhabited the area around the Ardennes.

Two individuals, Indutiomarus and Cingetorix, were at war with each other in a bid to become the tribe's leader. Cingetorix was loyal to Caesar whereas Indutiomarus was not. It was therefore important to resolve this conflict before taking the bulk of his army on an invasion of Britain. Once they saw what they were up against, both protagonists sued for peace and Caesar for his part ensured that there would be no uprising in his absence by taking two hundred hostages, including Indutiomarus' son and all his relatives. He told Indutiomarus and other rebels within the tribe that they should support Cingetorix and they agreed to do so, although there was a lot of resentment amongst them.

Once this situation had been resolved, Caesar returned to Portus Itius with the legions. All the ships, minus sixty, were now fully equipped and ready to go to sea. Caesar had summoned the leaders of all the local tribes to Portus Itius as well as 4,000 cavalry from tribes all over Gaul who he intended to use as mercenaries. To ensure that there would be no trouble from local tribes whilst he and his legions were in Britain, he decided to take with him all the hostages he had accumulated so far, together with the leaders of Gallic tribes who he felt were not fully loyal. This was clearly a very shrewd move to ensure stability in Gaul.

However, one of these leaders, called Dumnorix, of the Aedui tribe from what is now central France whom Caesar knew to be a political intriguer, tried everything he could to avoid being one of the leaders taken as a hostage to Britain. He used all sorts of arguments, saying that he was unused to sailing and afraid of the seas, and when that didn't work, said that he couldn't go to Britain for religious reasons. Caesar was determined not to leave Dumnorix behind and so Dumnorix then started stirring up trouble amongst all the other tribal chiefs who Caesar was taking as hostages to Britain. In particular, Dumnorix spread a rumour that Caesar wanted to kill all the hostages but that he didn't want to do so in Gaul where their tribesmen could see it happening, so he was taking them to Britain to kill them there.

Caesar had a high regard for the Aedui tribe so, when he got to hear of Dumnorix's plans, rather than punish him, he tried to defuse the situation.

Meanwhile, bad weather had delayed the sailing but when it improved, Caesar ordered his infantry and the cavalry to start loading the ships. However, while this was going on, Dumnorix took some of the Aeduan cavalry and headed for home. When Caesar was informed of this, he sent a detachment of cavalry to pursue Dumnorix with orders to bring him back to the port. Dumnorix resisted and waved his sword, shouting at his followers to protect him. At this point, Caesar realised it would be unsafe to travel to Britain leaving a potential rebel like Dumnorix behind and he ordered Dumnorix to be killed. After Dumnorix had been killed, the Aeduan cavalry who had followed him returned to the Roman camp.

Once this potential revolt had been dealt with, Caesar's fleet set sail. He left one of his generals – Labienus – with three legions and 2,000 cavalry to guard the port, and to deal with any problems which might arise in Gaul whilst Caesar was away.

The invading army consisted of five legions, and the other half of the cavalry; two thousand horsemen in total. They sailed at sunset with a light south-westerly wind. However, at midnight the wind dropped, and they floated along on the tide. After a while they found they were leaving Britain behind on the port side. The current then changed and rowing hard, they reached the part of Britain that Caesar says was where he had seen the best landing places the previous year.

When they did reach the coast of Britain, unlike the previous year, the enemy was nowhere to be seen. Caesar later discovered from prisoners he had taken, that the Britons were scared stiff when they saw that the size of the fleet was massively larger than that the year before and they had therefore run off to hide on higher ground. In total, over 800 ships were in the fleet.

The army disembarked, and Caesar chose a site for his camp. Having taken a few prisoners, he quizzed them and learned where the enemy had gone. He set out at midnight on an overnight march leaving a smaller force in charge of guarding the camp. After they had gone about twelve miles, they sighted the enemy who then advanced to a river with their cavalry and chariots and tried to bar the way by attacking from higher ground.

The Britons were seen off by the cavalry and they formed up in a well-prepared hill fort with entrances which they had barred with felled trees, from which they attacked the Romans from time to time. The Roman army eventually took the hill fort by attacking, using the testudo technique of locking their shields together both frontally and over their heads. By this means they took the hill fort with only a few men wounded, and set about converting it into their own camp, which would be their first marching camp. The troops wanted to chase after the Britons, but Caesar ordered them not to do so because he wanted to continue fortifying his camp.

The troops did pursue the enemy the following day but while this was going on, dispatch riders arrived to tell Caesar that his fleet had been damaged during the night by a massive storm and that a lot of the damage had resulted from ships running into each other.

When he got back to his base camp on the coast, he found that forty ships were a total loss and all the rest of the ships would need work doing on them to ensure they would be seaworthy.

He immediately gathered together all the skilled workmen in his army, sent to the continent for more, and left a message with Labienus at Portus Itius to build as many new ships as he could using his legionaries.

Lastly, Caesar decided to beach the ships to ensure they would not be damaged in the future and he had them hauled up onto dry land as near as possible to his camp and then ordered the ships and the camp together to be strongly fortified.

When he was satisfied, he left the base camp under the control of the same troops who had been left to guard the port before and returned to the temporary camp he had constructed before the storm had diverted him.

When he got back, he found that the Britons had swelled their numbers and that the enemy was now under the direction of Cassivellaunus, the chief of the Catuvellauni. Cassivellaunus had been continually at war with the other British tribes but faced with the threat of the Romans, they had all agreed to band together and to give the leadership to Cassivellaunus.

Cassivellaunus' headquarters was eighty miles from the coast beyond the Thames.

At this point in his narrative, Caesar takes time out to give a description of the Ancient Britons and their way of life.

He states that Britain had a large population and that there were very many homesteads. There were lots of natural resources, particularly gold and iron. Cattle were kept and so were geese, but the Britons made it unlawful to eat geese. There was plenty of timber and he declared that the climate was better than Gaul particularly that the cold was less severe.

The island, he wrote, was in the shape of a triangle and one corner of the triangle is present-day Kent, which was the landing place for almost all the ships coming from Gaul.

The most civilised inhabitants were those in Kent and these inhabitants were the ones who were most similar to the Gauls. The main diet of the Britons was milk and meat. They dressed in skins and painted their bodies with woad which gave them a blue colour. They shaved the whole of their bodies except their head and their upper lips.

Wives were shared between ten to twelve men, generally brothers, fathers and sons but the offspring of these relationships were regarded as the children of the man the woman first had had a relationship with.

Returning to his account, Caesar says that the Roman cavalry was attacked constantly on its march by the British cavalry and charioteers but that the Romans beat the enemy at all times, driving them into the woods and hills. Things quietened down but suddenly, while the troops were off guard fortifying the camp, the enemy dashed out of the woods and attacked the legionaries on guard at an outpost beyond the entrance to the camp.

Caesar sent two cohorts (each similar to a modern-day battalion) to relieve the troops on the outpost but they found the tactics of the British hard to deal with and were effectively beaten. During that battle, which could be seen from the camp, a military tribune, (a senior officer) Quintus Laberius Durus was killed. Caesar sent more cohorts and the Britons were eventually beaten off.

The Romans found it difficult fighting the Britons, partly because they were weighed down by their armour but also because the Britons engaged in guerrilla warfare and the Romans were more used to fighting pitched battles.[3]

The day after the skirmish in which Quintus Laberius Durus was killed, the Britons took to the hills some distance from the camp and in the morning, small groups attacked the cavalry on the march.

At midday, Caesar sent three legions out on a foraging expedition under Gaius Trebonius. Suddenly the Britons swooped down from the hills and attacked the legions. The legionaries counter-attacked and the Britons fled. The cavalry then pursued the enemy, a great many of whom were killed. Caesar says that this battle resulted in all the tribes who had joined under Cassivellaunus dispersing and that as a result the Britons never again fought as a mass army.

It becomes clear that Caesar was angry at Cassivellaunus' involvement and determined to beard that lion in his den. Accordingly, he led his army to the Thames in order to cross over into Cassivellaunus' territory. Caesar says that the Thames was fordable at one point only and even there with difficulty.

When he reached the Thames, he could see that a large enemy force was lined up on the opposite bank and that stakes had been fixed on the bank to hinder the Romans. He also heard that the Britons had put stakes in the river bed. Caesar sent the cavalry across first and then the legionaries. The legionaries waded across the river even though they were up to their necks in water. The combination of the legionaries and the cavalry overpowered the enemy and they fled from the river bank.

Cassivellaunus now decided that the only way of defence was to engage in guerrilla tactics. He disbanded his army and retained only 4,000 charioteers. He hid his charioteers in amongst the local inhabitants, together with their cattle, along the route Caesar took. The Britons only attacked the Romans when they broke formation to go foraging whereupon, Cassivellenaunus would send his charioteers out by established lanes and pathways known to them. These attacks were very fierce, and they forced Caesar to keep his cavalry with the legions and to limit the extent to which the legionaries could engage in pillaging and burning.

During the march, the Trinovantes tribe sent envoys to Caesar undertaking to surrender and obey Caesar's orders. The Trinovantes were no friends of Cassivellaunus, who had killed their king, his son, Mandubracius, having to flee to Gaul, coming under Caesar's protection. The envoys asked for Mandubracius to be allowed to return to become their leader. Seeing an opportunity to break up the British tribes, Caesar agreed to the Trinovantes request – though at the same time he demanded forty hostages and grain for his troops. The Trinovantes duly sent the hostages and the grain.

Once it became known that the Trinovantes had secured Caesar's protection, many other tribes sent envoys and surrendered to Caesar.

Around this time Caesar learnt he was now not far from Cassivellaunus' headquarters in the powerfully-built hill fort at Wheathampstead. Despite its strong defences, the Romans attacked Cassivellaunus' fortress on two sides and overcame the British who broke and fled. Many of those who tried to escape were captured and killed. Caesar found a large quantity of cattle in the fortress which would no doubt have helped to feed his troops.

Meanwhile, Cassivellaunus, never one to give up, sent messengers to Kent ordering four kings of the region to make a surprise attack on the Roman's shore camp. This attack was quickly and easily put down by the Romans and many of the enemy were killed. The Romans captured one of the tribal leaders, Lugotorix.

Once news of this disaster reached Cassivellaunus, he realised the game was up and sued for peace. Caesar decided to accept Cassivellaunus surrender as he was becoming concerned in case an uprising might occur in Gaul and autumn was fast approaching and he needed to return to Gaul.

Having succeeded in defeating Cassivellaunus, Caesar demanded hostages from him, an annual tribute to be paid to the Roman government and an undertaking that Cassivellaunus would not harm Mandubracius or the Trinovantes.

Once the hostages were delivered, Caesar led his army back to the coast. Many ships had been repaired but virtually none of the new ships or ships repaired in Gaul which had been sent to Britain unladen from the continent, actually arrived.

Nevertheless, the sea was calm. He set sail late in the evening, at a date which is assumed to be late September, and landed back in Gaul at dawn. As Caesar had a large number of hostages it took two trips for his entire force to be shipped back to the continent.

Chapter Two

Rome in the First Century BC

R ome and its empire lasted for over 1,000 years but almost certainly the most influential period of its existence was the 100 years of the first century BC. It was at the beginning of this century that Julius Caesar was born in 100 BC, living until he was assassinated in 44 BC.

The first century BC was a period of enlightenment in the history of Rome and a time of extreme change, which saw Rome abandon its republican status and ultimately become ruled by an emperor. By the beginning of the first century BC, Rome had acquired a massive empire and, by the end of the century, it had conquered almost all of what was then the known world.

Tradition states that Rome was founded on 21 April 753 BC by Romulus who had murdered his brother Remus, both of whom had been abandoned and were suckled by a she wolf. This is, of course, entirely mythical. Rome would have been a little village, or more likely a collection of villages, in the mid-eighth century BC, but one that maintained some form of independent status. It would have been one amongst many similar little village states but this one managed to grow into one of the greatest empires there has ever been.

Rome was ideally positioned.It was situated near the coast, thus enabling water-borne communication up and down the Tyrrhenian Sea. There were the seven hills, any of which would have made a ready site for a hill fort and of course running through it was the River Tiber which was perfect for transport and inland communication.

However, above all, there are two main reasons behind the growth of Rome and how it rose to conquer the known world.

The first is that Rome was unusual amongst its other contemporary city states in that it was a democracy ruled not by an autocrat but by its people, although for most of the time not all the people. Also, once it had ceased to be a monarchy, its rulers, the consuls, only held office for one year and therefore, as a consequence, consuls could readily be held accountable.

Couple this with another quality unique to Rome, its egalitarianism and diversity and the result was an entirely modern society in which, in general, all its people could feel comfortable and safe.

This egalitarianism extended to the fact that progressively, the populations of those territories conquered by Rome were invariably ultimately granted Roman citizenship. There was even a halfway house to Roman citizenship, which was called Latin Rights, which was named after the neighbouring Latin tribe who were first given these rights by Rome.

Also, as Rome progressively conquered other territories it became mandatory that those territories provide soldiers for the Roman Army. As a result, Rome was able to increase the size of its armies each time it conquered a territory, enabling it to have a larger army to conquer the next territory, and so on.

With few exceptions, amongst which was Claudius' later conquest of Britain This 500 years of republican democracy, stretching from 509 BC to 27 BC was the era when Rome created its empire.

For the first 250 years or so, following its purported foundation, Rome was ruled by a succession of kings, seven in all. These kings were elected by the Roman senate and did not inherit the throne as the later emperors often did.

Some of the elements of the later Roman constitution were formulated during the reign of the kings but by and large in the 250 or so years that they held the throne, they did not really achieve very much.

The reign of the kings finally came to an end in 509 BC. The last king, Tarquin, known as Tarquin the Proud and also Tarquin Superbus, became increasingly tyrannical and the populace reached a point where it had had enough.

Tarquin had seized the throne from his predecessor Servius Tullius, who was then murdered by Tarquin's associates. Tarquin refused to bury Servius, murdered a number of senators who were loyal to Servius and then proceeded to rule Rome in an autocratic and dictatorial manner. As a result, the population became increasingly unhappy with its king.

Like so many tyrants in history, Tarquin kept up a continuous process of building and rebuilding which placed a great burden upon the population and further enhanced his unpopularity.[1]

In 510 BC, Tarquin decided to go to war with a local tribe, the Rutuli, who were based to the southeast of Rome. This tribe was very wealthy and the principal reason for the war was that Tarquin wanted to get his hands on their wealth.

Meanwhile, Tarquin's son, Sextus, was sent by his father to Collatia, a town to the east of Rome to meet with the local governor. Whilst there, Sextus raped the Governor's wife Lucretia who felt such shame that she committed suicide.

By that time, the people had had enough, and the Romans rose up, led by Lucius Junius Brutus and Publius Valerius. It was decided that Tarquin and his family should be expelled from Rome for good. Lucius Junius Brutus was supposedly an ancestor of Brutus, one of the assassins of Julius Caesar.

A number of battles were fought between Rome and Tarquin in which Tarquin had the aid of some of Rome's neighbouring states but he was finally defeated and was sent into exile. Rome was then ruled by two consuls although they were not called as such until later. Initially they were called praetors.

One result of the overthrow of Tarquin was that forever after during the republic the concept of kingship was an anathema to the Romans.[2] So began the Republic, throughout the period of which Rome steadily developed its systems of government based on its own version of democracy.

The first 100 years of the republic were somewhat uneventful, and Rome was only one of many small city states which existed throughout Italy at the time; but at the beginning of the fourth century BC, two significant events occurred. The first was a victory by the Romans over a neighbouring tribe of the Etruscans called the

Veii. This victory, however, was short lived, as immediately after defeating the Veii, Rome was attacked by a tribe from Gaul called the Senones and a battle was fought at the Allia, a tributary of the Tiber, not far from Rome. The Roman armies were defeated by the Gauls who then set about sacking Rome itself. The Romans offered the Senones a ransom to leave the city but later reneged on it. This resulted in a further battle with the Senones and on that occasion, the Roman army prevailed and the Senones were defeated.

The sacking of the city was a deep shock to the Romans and they immediately set about rebuilding the parts of the city that had been destroyed and, most importantly, they constructed a massive wall around the Rome to ensure such an invasion should not occur again. Remains of that wall can still be seen today.

This event marked a low point in the history of Rome and it is an attractive idea to think that the collective memory of this event may have influenced Caesar in deciding to conquer Gaul in the first century BC in order, to some extent, to right a wrong.

In the main, the fortunes of Rome began to steadily improve following this humiliating setback, and by the early third century BC, conquests by Rome had resulted in virtually the whole of Italy falling under its control. Roman forces then began the conquest of Sicily, expelling the Carthaginians in the process. The Carthaginians were a long-established nation based in North Africa which had dominated trade in the mid to western Mediterranean. They were major rivals to Rome and had developed as a nation in a way similar to that of Rome. Like the Romans, the Carthaginians were also conquerors and had acquired an empire which included most of the coast of north Africa, part of Sicily, and a large part of southern Spain.

In some respects, the wars between the Romans and the Carthaginians was a classic battle of the titans. Whoever won would be master of the Mediterranean.

This conflict lasted for over a hundred years starting in 264 BC and ending in 146 BC. It involved three phases, known as the three Punic wars, the second of which involved the famous campaign when Hannibal crossed the Alps with his army complete with elephants.

The last Punic war involved a three-year siege and the eventual capture of Carthage. The Romans then burnt Carthage to the ground and enslaved its entire population. Carthage and the Carthaginians were no more.

Carthage was not the only military success for Rome in the period during which the Punic wars were being fought. From 214 BC to 148 BC, Rome was fighting wars in Greece, principally against the kingdom of Macedonia, by far the largest state in Greece. When Macedonia was finally conquered in 148 BC, Rome occupied Macedonia and split it into two Roman provinces, Achaea and Epirus. Rome had become the dominant force in the Mediterranean and could steadily increase its empire without hindrance from any other major power.

The sack of Carthage happened in 146 BC, the Macedonian wars having been won two years earlier. When Caesar was born in 100 BC, he would have been born into a world where the pride and prestige of Rome had never been higher. The memory of the victories over Carthage and Macedonia would have been fresh in the collective memory of Rome and the Roman population, and as Caesar was growing up, there would be many old people around who would remember the events of 146 BC. Caesar would undoubtedly have spent his formative years basking in the pride of a nation which had conquered the whole of the Mediterranean hinterland.

The defeat of Carthage and that of Macedonia were the trigger for the launch of the greatest century in Roman history, the century beginning in 100 BC, the year Julius Caesar was born, and a century ultimately dominated by him.

The first century BC would undoubtedly have been a period of consolidation and adjustment for Rome and its people – adjustment principally to the need to rule vast territories and to be the capital city and the centre of the world as it was then known, though the territory it controlled was much less than would be the case later. There would undoubtedly have been a collective feeling of invincibility on the part of Rome and its people. Inevitably this would manifest itself in the desire to continue its process of conquest and this attitude would have been instilled in the mind of many Romans and particularly those of the ruling classes and especially in a young man setting out in the world, one Gaius Julius Caesar.

The early part of the century was dominated by wars against Mithridates, the King of Pontus, an area which was situated in what is now modern Turkey. In some respects, these wars were a departure from the two massive wars of the previous century against Carthage and Macedonia in that Rome was engaged in preventing Mithridates from attempting to win back Roman conquered lands in Greece. Rome was now entering a period when not only would it conquer new lands, but it would be called upon from time to time to ensure that its empire remained intact.

Like the Punic wars, there were three distinct wars against Mithridates covering the period from 88 BC to 63 BC and various generals conducted these on Rome's behalf, the first being Marius. The last war against Mithridates was won under the generalship of Pompey, a friend and associate of Caesar both of whom would, in due course, go on to form a triumvirate of power with another general and politician, Marcus Licinius Crassus.

As the new century progressed, the struggle for power by various individuals began to challenge the old order of the republic and this process continued as time passed. For example, Consuls should only hold office for one year and yet Marius held the consulship on seven occasions.

A civil war erupted in 88 BC. Although the senate had awarded the generalship of the war against Mithridates to Marius, it had previously offered it to another general, Lucius Cornelius Sulla. As a result, Sulla took his army and invaded and occupied the city of Rome. He became a virtual dictator but eventually retired to his country home where he died peacefully. Life then returned to normal in Rome. Surprisingly, Rome held a funeral for him which was as magnificent as those which would be held later for emperors. Rome and Roman rule was changing, and the old order was collapsing.

Next came an event which was entirely unexpected, which was a revolt by the slaves of Rome organised by one of their number called Spartacus. The revolt lasted from 73 BC to 71 BC when Spartacus was finally defeated and killed, although his body was never found. Six thousand members of his army were crucified along the Appian way, the main road out of Rome to the south.

What was becoming clear was that holding together the vast empire of Rome was becoming more and more difficult and what seems to have been emerging was the reality that the only way to do so successfully would be by having autocratic rule.

It was into this environment that Caesar's power and influence was emerging. This somewhat chaotic system of government by the Republic which was progressively being undermined by power-grabs allowed a man like Caesar to get away with doing what he wanted, particularly as regards his campaigns in Gaul and ultimately allowing him to assume absolute power.

Even so, in this century of massive change in the Roman world, the ultimate blueprint for governance had not emerged and would not do so until the start of the age of emperors. As a result, the establishment was not yet ready for full autocratic rule and Caesar paid the price in due course by his assassination.

Chapter Three

Caesar the Man

Introduction

What we know of the character of the man who invaded Britain in 55 BC is that he was an incredibly complex person and at the same time both a genius and an enigma.

He shares the extraordinary skill of the multi-talented genius of which there have been few in history. Leonardo da Vinci comes to mind as also does Winston Churchill. These people excelled in more than one field as did Caesar. Julius Caesar was an outstanding military leader, a consummate politician, a renowned orator and a writer whose prose has been heralded throughout history. He also wrote poetry and studied science.[1]

Caesar has been lauded throughout the last 2000 years by a large majority of the great and good who have lived since he was around. He gave his name to the title of the leader of the united German empire, the Kaiser and to the Czars who led the mighty Russian empire.

Boswell, in his life of Johnson, which is considered one of the finest biographies in the English language, calls Caesar the greatest man of any age.[2] And of course, William Shakespeare wrote a play about him.

Yet in all, Caesar has come into much criticism particularly about his ruthlessness, perceived cruelty and egotism. We need to try to identify what it was about Caesar that made him so great and which resulted in him being hailed as one of the greatest and for some *the* greatest man in history.

Youth training and education

Gaius Julius Caesar was born in July 100 BC, the son of Gaius Julius Caesar and Aurelia Cotta. Gaius was his forename, Caesar was his surname and Romans also had a family name and this was Julius.

His father was a patrician and those were the aristocracy of Rome but his mother's family, the Aurelii Cottae, were originally plebeians, the non-aristocratic class. The Julians were, to some extent on the wane, in the Roman hierarchy and the Aurelii Cottae were an up and coming clan which had produced four consuls, one of whom was Caesar's grandfather. As a result, the Aurelii Cottae were a useful connection for Caesar's political career that was to develop later.

Caesar's father's sister had married Gaius Marius, the successful general who had been elected consul an unprecedented seven times Undoubtedly Marius would have been a considerable influence on the young Caesar during his formative years. Also, the fame which Marius had achieved would have served to enhance the standing of Caesar's family.

Education for young Roman aristocrats when Caesar was growing up consisted to a large extent in learning fighting techniques and other military matters. In addition, Caesar would have learned horsemanship.

At the age of fifteen, a boy would finally be allowed to wear a male toga. It seems that fifteen was a significant age at which a boy became a man in the eyes of Roman society. As part of his introduction into society, Caesar was taken to the forum and to the senate to hear debates and would have been introduced to various politicians. All this was the beginning of grooming for a life in politics, which was the only real option in Rome at the time for a patrician lad from a leading family.

Once a boy had reached his late teens and early twenties, it was normal for him to serve a year in the army, which Caesar duly did. For his actions in rescuing a colleague in a battle during his military service he was decorated with the award of the citizen's crown, which consisted of a wreath of oak leaves which he was entitled to wear on special state occasions.

After leaving the army, Caesar then went to study in Rhodes in 75 BC.

As a youth, he was very much a lady's man and according to his biographer, Suetonius, he had many affairs. One of these affairs which developed into a deep love, was with the mother of Marcus Brutus, who would later be one of his assassins.

During this formative period, Caesar found himself becoming more and more at variance with the established political status quo of Rome and yet that political society was very closeted. Challenging the status quo meant becoming an outsider and this was a difficult position to take. Despite this, Caesar was able to continuously enlarge his network of political friends and contacts not only those from within his own family but throughout Rome.

Between 88 and 80 BC, a period during which Caesar was reaching adulthood, Rome was rocked by a massive civil war between Sulla on the one hand and Cinna and Caesar's uncle Marius on the other. After many years of fighting, during which both sides were alternatively in the ascendant, Sulla won the war and became dictator. A dictator in Rome was not how we regard them today, it was a temporary position to enable effective government in times of war.

It was during the civil war, when Caesar was still fifteen, that his father died. Then at the age of sixteen, Caesar married Cinna's daughter, Cornelia.

As a result of the outcome of the civil war, he was in a very precarious position, being a nephew of Marius and the son-in-law of Cinna.

When Sulla entered Rome, he hunted down his enemies and 3,000 of them were killed. Caesar had to go into hiding, fleeing from one hiding place to another. While he was in hiding, he was found by a patrol during the night and the only way Caesar could get away was to bribe them.

Curiously, despite the fact that Marius was Caesar's uncle, it is clear that Caesar admired Sulla. This was probably the first time that Caesar showed his later character of ruthlessly supporting whoever was in power in order to further his own ends.

Sulla ended his life as the ruler of Rome, and the fact that there are parallels in Sulla's power and how it was achieved through force, with the way in which Caesar behaved when he eventually came to control Rome, indicates that Caesar was probably carefully studying the way in which Sulla was operating.

After 80 BC, Caesar once again joined the army and sometime during the 70s Cornelia gave birth to a daughter Julia.

On leaving the army, Caesar decided to go to Rhodes to study rhetoric under Apollonius Molon. However, on the way there, he was captured by pirates who demanded a ransom of twenty talents. Showing his arrogance and egotism, he asked them if they realised who they had captured and told them that they were undervaluing him. He said they should demand fifty talents.

The ransom was duly paid, whereupon Caesar chartered a boat, recruited a small force on the promise that they could have all the booty they captured, including the fifty talents and then proceeded to capture the pirates. In an early showing of Caesar's ruthlessness towards his enemy when he chose to do so, he had the pirates strangled then crucified.

Hardly had he started his studies in Rhodes when Mithridates the king of Pontus crossed into Asia Minor and attempted to persuade the province of Asia to leave the Roman Empire. Caesar, on his own volition, raised an army locally and prevented a number of towns which had been settled by Romans from going over to Mithridates. Caesar was aware of the numbers of Romans massacred under Mithridates in previous skirmishes and it is clear that he wanted to protect Romans who had settled locally.

The fact that Caesar raised this army and succeeded in achieving his objectives without anyone asking or instructing him to do so is extraordinary. It showed a care for Rome and its citizens and marked the beginning of Caesar's generalship. He was only twenty-six at the time.

He was regarded as a hero in Rome and as a result he was appointed as a pontifex, a priestly appointment but one of administration only. He had won friends and influenced people and was laying the groundwork for his rise in Roman politics.

Political Rise

It was at or around the age of twenty-five that Caesar started taking his political career seriously. At twenty-six he was achieving fame in the wars against Mithridates. What is not clear is whether Caesar's successes as a general were achieved in order to further his political ambitions or were those political ambitions merely to seek high office which would bring with it the governorship of Roman provinces. Of course, also, provincial governorship brought with it the opportunity to plunder those provinces for the acquisition of wealth.

Put another way was it wealth Caesar sought or power? The truth is probably that the two objectives were interdependent and that in reality he wanted both but above all both were the means to enable him to achieve fame and this he coveted more than anything.

One problem for anyone wanting to rise up in Roman politics was that there was a minimum age at which a man could hold offices in the state. In reality, this meant that a political career could not take off until the age of thirty. Nevertheless, Caesar succeeded in getting elected to his first role as a military tribune in his late twenties.

After this, at the age of thirty, Caesar was appointed a Quaestor, the first rung on the ladder of Roman politics and the first step towards the office of consul.

As a Quaestor, he served on the Roman staff in the province of Hispania Ulterior in Spain. Suetonius states that when Caesar was in Gades, modern day Cadiz, he saw a monument to Alexander the Great and was moved by the fact that at the age of thirty one, Alexander had conquered the world. Caesar at the same age had thus far not achieved anything notable.

This may well have been Caesar's epiphany and that from then on, he would be driven to achieve at least as much as Alexander had.

Caesar's first wife Cornelia had died in 68 BC and he remarried in 67 BC, His second wife was Pompeia, who was the granddaughter of Sulla who had ruled Rome in the 80s and who had been the sworn enemy of Caesar's family. It may be that this was Caesar cosying up to the family that had opposed his and forming some sort of grand alliance.

Around this time, pirates were becoming an increasing nuisance in the Mediterranean. The senate wanted to appoint Pompey who was one of the most powerful men in Rome to lead an army to rid the Mediterranean of these pirates and Caesar gave his support. Once again, he was making sure he was allying himself to those who had power in Rome.

In order to progress in Roman politics, it was necessary to influence the electorate and the way to do that was to provide them with lavish games, banquets and theatre. The more lavish these events were, the more the general population favoured the aspirant politician.

Caesar held gladiatorial games and one in particular which he staged in memory of his father, had so many gladiators that the Senate set a limit on how many could perform. In response to the reduction in the number of gladiators he was allowed to field, Caesar had them all dressed in armour made of solid silver.

This and other extravagances resulted in Caesar becoming heavily in debt. However, despite this, on discovering that the post of Pontifex Maximus had become vacant, he borrowed as much as he could to bribe the electors and was so much in debt that he said to his mother on leaving home to go to the election that he would either return as Pontifex Maximus or not return at all. In other words, he would have to flee the country.

In the event, he won the election with an overwhelming majority.

This election put him in the front rank of the senate and his goal now was to be elected consul. Two consuls were elected each year to serve for a year and were effectively the rulers of Rome.

Shortly afterwards, Caesar discovered that his wife had smuggled a man, Publius Clodius Pulcher in the disguise of a woman into a secret women only religious ceremony. Although it was never established whether an affair had taken place, Caesar divorced Pompeia, famously stating that Caesar's wife must be above suspicion.

In 61 BC Caesar was appointed as governor of the province of Hispania Ulterior in South Eastern Spain. In Spain, he campaigned against local tribes and conquered much of the country and was declared Imperator by his men. This was a title given to Roman generals to honour their victory in battles. In addition, the senate awarded him a triumph, which was a triumphal procession of a successful general through the streets of Rome.

Although delighted to be awarded a triumph, this presented Caesar with a problem. The elections for the consulship were imminent and there was a law which stated that a general could not enter Rome until the day of his triumph. The date set for the triumph would be after the elections for the post of consul. Caesar had to make a decision and as becoming consul was his primary objective he relinquished his triumph and announced his candidacy for the election.

In 60 BC, he was elected consul for the following year and immediately made a pact with Pompey, the most influential man in Rome and Crassus the richest. Crassus had been the general who had conquered the army of the rebel slave Spartacus. This created what became known as the Triumvirate and although Caesar had a fellow consul Marcus Calpurnius Bibulus, he was effectively the sole ruler together with his two partners in the Triumvirate.

Asinius Pollio, who wrote a history of the overthrow of the Roman republic, took the view that 60 BC marked the beginning of the end of the republic.

59 BC was a turning point in the history of Rome. Although there were two consuls, Caesar's fellow consul Bibulus was effectively powerless. Cicero, who was a leading senator, said that he could not trust Caesar, and a joke going around the city was that Rome was being governed by Julius and Caesar.[3]

Caesar was becoming increasingly ruthless. He had one of his arch rivals, Cato arrested for opposing a law which Caesar wanted to introduce, although he did release him later.

Shortly after becoming consul, Caesar remarried for a third time. This time his wife was Calpurnia, the daughter of Lucius Calpurnius Piso who was a supporter of Caesar.

Caesar's period as Consul included his introduction of a law which regulated the entirety of the provincial administration, a law which survived well into the subsequent imperial period.

As Consul, he was appointed to govern Cisalpine Gaul, modern day Northern Italy.

There is a probability that the main reason he sought the consulship was to ensure that he gained the governorship of an important province as this would set him on the road to achieving his objective of emulating his hero Alexander.

In the autumn of 59 BC he had his new father in law Lucius Calpurnius Piso appointed as one of the two consuls for the following year.

He was now about to start his campaigns in Gaul.

The campaigns in Gaul

Caesar took up his governorship in Gaul but ensured that he continued to keep in touch with Rome and able to influence politics at home. For this reason, he maintained an office in the city and had two secretaries back there who worked for him.[4]

Roman society was undergoing massive change and the established order was slowly disintegrating. There were lawless gangs patrolling the streets.

However important it was to keep a hand on events in Rome, he was happiest when he was with his soldiers on campaign. These were some of the finest soldiers in the Roman army and they were highly skilled and highly trained.

On taking up his post, he immediately encountered a threat from the Helvetii a tribe bordering on Cisalpine Gaul. He clearly needed to counter this threat.

Rome had laws that forbade governors from waging war unless it was necessary to protect Roman interests. Clearly the threat from the Helvetii came into this category but as we shall see, Caesar was not prepared to let things rest with merely defeating the Helvetii. He needed to ensure the stability of the whole of Gaul. He ultimately conquered all of Gaul and in addition suppressed any resistance in Britain.

Many in Rome felt that he had gone too far and that he had flouted the law preventing unrestricted war but by this time Caesar was powerful enough to ignore such views and he argued that he had needed to bring the whole of Gaul under Roman rule in order to ensure continuing peace. However, it did make him enemies in Rome.

Caesar had taken up his position in Cisalpine Gaul with a limited army and due to the threat from the Helvetii he left his deputy

Labienus to hold the fort while he returned to Rome to collect five new legions.

Caesar convincingly defeated the Helvetii and then went on to conquer the whole of Gaul.

His achievements in Gaul raised his status amongst all Romans despite the fact that he continued to have enemies at home.

Caesar wrote an account of his campaigns in Gaul, his famous De Bello Gallico. All military commanders were expected to write an account of their victories but Caesar used the language of everyday speech and created an account which has been praised ever since.

His account is matter of fact and contains no emotion. In it he demonstrates a determination and an ever present confidence.

An example of the absolute necessity for him to keep in touch with events back in Rome occurred in 56 BC. Caesar learnt that Lucius Domitius Ahenobarbus was planning to stand for the consulate in 55 BC and if elected intended to deprive Caesar of his command in Gaul.

Caesar fought his corner from the remote regions of Gaul and succeeded in defeating Ahenobarbus. To strengthen his control, he made a new alliance with his old partners in the triumvirate, Pompey and Crassus.

As a result of his actions he succeeded in having his command in Gaul extended by the senate until March 50 BC.

Caesar took on the Veneti a tribe in Brittany and defeated them at sea. During this campaign he found himself up against Britons who were acting as mercenaries for the Veneti. This was the first time he had come up against Britons and it probably cemented a determination in his mind that he would take his revenge on Britain in due course.

Having won the naval battle with the Veneti, Caesar had the whole of their senate executed to ensure they would not fight a war with Rome again.

It was this absolute ruthlessness almost driven by a sort of logical pragmatism that ensured that when Caesar had defeated a tribe, it should be a permanent defeat with no possibility of them attacking again.

Caesar intended to limit his conquests to Gaul but nevertheless, because German tribes had invaded Gaul and despite having tried to avoid entering German territory for long enough he eventually crossed the Rhine. It took him only ten days to build a bridge across the Rhine. The later crossing of the Thames therefore would not have fazed him at all.

The first invasion of Britain took place in 55 BC and in the autumn, on his return, he made a report to the senate. For the first time there was severe criticism of him for waging a war of conquest

This was whipped up by Caesar's main enemy within the senate, Marcus Porcius Cato Uticensis known as Cato the Younger. Despite Cato's intervention, the senate awarded Caesar an unprecedented twenty-day *Supplicatio,* which was a Roman thanksgiving for a great victory.

Meanwhile Caesar was indulging in lavish expenditure in Rome. He began to build a large covered voting hall of marble on the Campus Martius surrounded by a colonnade a mile long.

The funding for this was provided by the booty Caesar was extracting from Gaul. It is said that he often destroyed towns for their booty rather than to punish them for any infraction against Rome. Gaul was made to bleed and the effect on the Roman economy was such that the value of gold dropped by 25 percent due to the amount of it flooding into the city.[5]

During Caesar's second invasion of Britain in 54 BC, his beloved daughter Julia died. Also, at that time there was information reaching him that Pompey was seeking to establish a sole dictatorship in his name. These two events may well be why he left Britain when he did in late 54 BC although he had by then achieved his objective of subduing the British leader Cassivellaunus.

The two events were of course linked as Pompey had married Julia. Her death led to a process of estrangement between Caesar and Pompey. Crassus had died in battle and Pompey had left the Triumvirate and he now started to conspire against Caesar.

Caesar had conquered Gaul with such skill and energy that he had earned the reputation of being one of the greatest commanders of all time. Later he was hailed as such by Frederick the Great and Napoleon Bonaparte amongst others.[6]

It is said he radiated immense charisma, his soldiers loved him, especially his cheerfulness and the fact that if there were difficulties, as soon as Caesar appeared on the scene the tide would turn and the army would be victorious.

Not only was Caesar an outstanding general but in parallel with his military successes he continued to exercise political power in Rome albeit from a distance and he even found time to write his book *De analogia* in 54 BC on his way back to Gaul from Rome. The book is a plea for pure and accurate Latin and he dedicated it to Cicero as the father and master of Latin prose.

In the politics of Rome, Caesar increasingly felt that the senate and others were too preoccupied with trivia and this resulted in him tending to feel that he rose above them. As a consequence, there was an increasing opinion amongst a number of leading Romans that he was becoming arrogant and egotistical.

His final military act in Gaul was to put down a revolt by Vercingetorix, the king of the Arverni tribe in Southern Gaul who had succeeded in bringing together many of the tribes Caesar had already conquered into a last-ditch rebellion against Rome.

Although the war was not easy for Caesar to win, he did win in the end and Vercingetorix surrendered and was taken back to Rome as a hostage. Thereafter no tribes in Gaul ever revolted against Rome and it could look forward to the Romanisation of Gaul over the following half millennium.

The Civil War

Gaul was secure but Caesar was not. He found he had to fight a rearguard action in Rome as there were moves to strip him of his governorship and leave him as a private citizen. He knew that if this happened, he would be open to prosecution for starting the Gallic war without the consent of the senate.

The fundamental problem was that Caesar was an outsider. He didn't fit in with the established order in Rome. He had won fabulous victories and increased the Roman territory beyond measure and he had shown himself to be the greatest general in Rome, but Rome expected its citizens to conform. His ruthlessness, his superiority in dealing with anyone and the fact that he did not bow to the judgement of his peers, alienated him from the establishment.

Nonetheless, Caesar had immense respect for the structure of the republic and wished to preserve it even if he had little time for the people who populated that structure; the members of the senate. He made every effort to comply with the wishes of the senate and he wanted more than anything to avoid a civil war, but the bottom line was that he was determined to maintain his position and power and would not under any circumstances return to civilian life.

It became clear that Caesar was not going to get any of his demands met and, in the meantime, the senate declared a state of emergency. When this happened, it became obvious that a civil war was inevitable.

Caesar was still in his province of Cisalpine Gaul. The boundary between Cisalpine Gaul and the rest of Italy was the River Rubicon. Caesar knew that once he crossed that river with an army, the civil war would have started. After much agonising and soul searching he decided he had to cross the Rubicon, and this would be seen as an act of aggression against the Roman State.

The Roman poet, Lucan, wrote that on crossing the Rubicon, Caesar said 'here I leave the basis of law, dishonoured as it is'. He had clearly decided as a strong justification for his action that the Roman constitution was no longer sustainable.

The Consul, Marcellus, had given the responsibility of defending the state to Pompey, Caesar's old ally and having crossed the Rubicon, Caesar recognised that he needed to take the initiative immediately if he was going to defeat Pompey. He very quickly took a number of towns in Italy whilst in the meantime Pompey had decided to abandon Rome and leave it effectively as an open city.

Cicero said that the war was basically a war between Pompey and Caesar for each to obtain an autocracy. It was, he said, an act of madness.

For Caesar, it was not simply a defensive war to ensure he would not be indicted by the senate on the basis of an unauthorised war in Gaul, nor was it simply for the purpose of seeking power. No, it was started by Caesar because here was a man who had enlarged the Roman Empire by achieving extraordinary success on the battlefield and yet who was not only not being recognised for his achievements in Rome but also being vilified.

It soon became clear to Pompey and the senate that Caesar was winning the war and as a result they offered Caesar everything he had demanded, Pompey would leave the country and go to Spain and in return Caesar should withdraw from the Roman territory he had occupied. Not surprisingly, Caesar did not trust Pompey and the senate and rejected their offer.

At this point, in an act of absolute treachery, Caesar's effective second-in-command, Titus Labienus defected to Pompey. It was Titus Labienus who had held the base camp for Caesar in Gaul when Caesar invaded Britain. This action prompted Pompey to some extent to change his tactics. However, eventually this did no good, basically because Pompey was up against a far superior general.

Caesar fought and won against an army led by Ahenobarbus, fighting on behalf of Pompey at Corfinium, east of Rome and he took the town. The enemy troops and the population of the town expected a wholesale slaughter as this was what had happened to captive troops and towns in the last civil war of the 80s under Sulla.

Caesar however employed a clever tactic. He pardoned all the enemy troops and caused no bloodshed in the town. After all these were all Roman citizens. This act of clemency was a smart thing to do, was consistent with his reasons for going to war and was a measure of his statesmanship. Significantly, it was also something that only monarchs generally did. Clemency contrasted with the style of Pompey and the old republic which operated on the basis of cruelty.

In due course Caesar had conquered the whole of Italy and with hardly any fighting. Pompey however had fled abroad, and the war would not be won until he had been defeated. Consequently, Caesar would have to follow Pompey abroad but unfortunately, he had no navy. Pompey had control of the sea and Caesar had no ships.

In the meantime, Caesar entered Rome as the victor and set about a hearts-and-minds policy. He addressed the people and promised to ensure the delivery of food supplies and even promised to distribute money. To enable this to happen, he assembled the senators, at least those who hadn't left when Rome had been declared an open city, and demanded they hand over the treasury, saying he needed the money to fund his fight against Pompey. Not surprisingly, the senators refused, but he took it anyway

He left Marcus Aemilius Lepidus an ally of his in charge of the city, with the title of Dictator, and left to pursue Pompey and to bring an end to the civil war. Caesar campaigned against Pompey in Spain and he continued his policy of clemency. Whereas Pompey executed all the prisoners of war he took, Caesar returned Pompey's prisoners of war to him unharmed and spared the citizens of towns he had liberated. He even made his soldiers return plunder they had taken from Pompey's troops.

He defeated Pompey in Spain after a campaign lasting forty days and with hardly any bloodshed.

He returned to Rome and had himself elected consul. He was now in complete control of Rome, politically and militarily.

Caesar pursued Pompey to Greece and after a number of skirmishes, at some of which Pompey had the upper hand, the two armies met at Pharsalus in central Greece.

Pompey was comprehensively defeated and only just managed to escape with his life. He fled to Egypt hoping to find asylum there but as he stepped ashore, he was brutally assassinated.

The civil war was over. Caesar was now the undisputed ruler of Rome.

The Dictatorship

Following the battle of Pharsalus, Caesar sent news of his victory and instructions to Rome that he should be appointed Dictator for one year. In Rome, statues of Sulla and Pompey were removed and a monument was set up to 'Gaius Julius Caesar, son of Gaius, Pontifex Maximus, Imperator, Twice Consul, Manifest God, descended from Ares and Aphrodite and common deliverer of humanity.' No one in Rome dared to speak against Caesar because of the fear of informers but the reality was that Caesar had very few supporters in Rome.

When he heard that Pompey had gone to Egypt, Caesar crossed to Rhodes in order to sail to Alexandria. When he arrived, he was presented with Pompey's head which upset him. He had hoped to capture Pompey and then to pardon him. After all, they had been close friends and in-laws in the past.

The old Egyptian king had died and the country was now ruled jointly by Cleopatra and her brother Ptolemy XIII. Inevitably, as joint rulers, the two of them were at war with each other.

Caesar took up occupation in the royal palace and soon after arriving sent messages to both Cleopatra and her brother that he was prepared to help to settle their differences and that they should stop fighting, dismiss their armies and meet with him.

Ptolemy did not take up the invitation, but Cleopatra did. A small ship landed in the harbour at Alexandria one evening and a long bag tied up with straps was delivered to Caesar in the royal palace. The bag opened and out came Cleopatra attractively attired.

Caesar was utterly captivated with her. She was twenty-two, he was fifty-two and they were totally inseparable. They forged a strong relationship and spent days and nights together.

Caesar had arrived in Egypt with a small force and, despite the fact that he had succeeded in capturing Ptolemy, Ptolemy's army besieged the royal palace and Caesar was trapped inside for six months. Eventually, reinforcements arrived, Ptolemy was defeated and shortly afterwards died. In celebration, Caesar rode his troops on a victory parade through the former enemy's quarter of the city.

Amongst the reinforcements was a Jewish legion and as a reward, for sending them to assist him, Caesar rewarded Antipatros, the father of the later King Herod, with Roman Citizenship.

After spending an inordinate amount of time in Egypt with Cleopatra, during which he visited Alexander the Great's tomb, Caesar travelled to Syria to quell an uprising by Pharnaces, the son of Mithridates. He encountered Pharnaces and his army at Zela in modern day Turkey and very quickly defeated him, famously saying about the battle, *veni vidi vici* 'I came I saw I conquered'.

Caesar returned to Rome and called Cicero to meet with him. In view of all that had gone before, Cicero was understandably nervous at meeting Caesar again. He need not have been as Caesar greeted him as an old friend.

Caesar found he had spent all his fortune on the various wars he had won and demanded that the citizens of Rome and other towns should pay a tribute to him. He also sold off the property of those of his opponents who he had not pardoned. None of this was calculated to endear him to the average Roman citizen.

He was also under pressure from his troops who had not yet received their share of the spoils of his wars. As a result, they mutinied but he was able to talk them round to wait a little longer until he had celebrated his triumph. By dint of his oratory, he eventually had them totally on his side and he did not punish any of them for the mutiny.

By this time, Caesar was well into his fifties and had been fighting wars incessantly. He began to feel unwell from time to time and in his writings complained of his 'usual sickness'. It is believed that his 'usual sickness' was in fact epilepsy.[7]

Meanwhile, various malcontents, including two of Pompey's sons, had gathered an army in Africa and had allied themselves to a local king. Caesar left for Africa and despite inferior numbers on his part, succeeded in taking the town of Thapsus and decisively defeating the enemy. In no time, Caesar had gained control of all Roman Africa.

Unusually, on this occasion, he showed no clemency and all the enemy soldiers were massacred. It is possible that by now, Caesar was war-weary and perhaps beginning to lose his judgement.

When the war was over, he returned to Rome and invited Cleopatra to join him.

The senate appointed Caesar as dictator for ten years, but the reality was that he was now the ruler of Rome. However, the population remained unsure as to what Caesar wanted. He seemed to make it clear he did not want to be made king. He also insisted he should not be worshiped as a god. But what did he want to do with Rome? To some extent the Roman world was in a state of limbo waiting to see what would happen?

The Triumphs and celebrations for this war, as well as the wars in Egypt, Gaul and more recently in Pontus against Mithridates' son Pharnaces, were like nothing anyone had seen before, but still Caesar was not popular in Rome.

In the triumphs, a slave held a golden crown above his head and constantly whispered in his ear 'remember you are human'. In the theatre during the celebrations, one of the presentations was a demonstration of the tactics used by the British with their war chariots.

Finally, the booty long promised to the troops was shared out among them. However, Caesar gave a small amount to the urban populace. When the veterans protested at this, Caesar personally seized one of them and had him led away to be executed. This action, so uncharacteristic smacks of megalomania and leads us to wonder whether at this time, Caesar's mind was beginning to go. This possibility would also be consistent with his seeming inability to make up his mind where he wanted to stand within the hierarchy of the state, King, Emperor or Consul for life? All he seemed interested in was the acquisition of power for himself.

Following the death of Cato in the African Campaign, Cicero and Brutus wrote eulogies and Caesar responded by writing Anticato, a most obscene and virulent attack on the character of the man. Admittedly Cato had been a thorn in the side of Caesar for many years but what Caesar wrote was so out of character. We can only assume that by Cicero and Brutus praising Cato, Caesar saw this as an attack on him and if so this would show a degree of paranoia.

He lost the literary battle and the publication further alienated him from the population.

On the positive side it was during this period that Caesar ordered the Greek Mathematician Sosigenes to design a new calendar and the result was the Julian calendar, aspects of which are still in use today.

Caesar's behaviour continued to be erratic. Anyone who challenged his authority would incur his wrath and he started acting arbitrarily with the way in which the republic operated. In addition, he was becoming more and more ruthless. On one occasion he said people should take what he said as the law.

He made sure his veteran soldiers were given land and were comfortably settled and to make sure they were all protected, he liberally gave out the Latin Right, a precursor to full citizenship to all and sundry.

The city continued to heap awards on him, but all the time he was becoming more and more unpopular. He was given the unique distinction of being able to be buried within the city whereas all Romans were buried outside the city gates.

Caesar had had a bodyguard for some time but suddenly he decided to dismiss it and despite advice from many of his friends he refused to reinstate it. Caesar was extending his power to such an extent that many people feared that he would become a full-blown tyrant. As a result, a conspiracy started with a view to assassinating him and the number of conspirators reached sixty.

On 15th March 44 BC, the Ides of March, they took action and Caesar was stabbed to death in the senate.

There is a theory that Brutus, one of the assassins was in fact Caesar's illegitimate son. Indeed, Suetonius suggests that far from saying 'et tu Brute' as Shakespeare has it, he actually said 'and you my son'.[8]

After his death, Caesar was hailed as a God and had a temple built for him in the Forum at Rome.

So ended the remarkable life of a remarkable man. A man with human frailties like all of us, but a man who changed Rome and the Roman world for ever and who influenced Europe for decades afterwards.

Chapter Four

The Roman Army in the First Century BC

The constitution of the Roman army went through three distinct phases from the origins of Rome to the end of the western empire in the fifth century AD.[1] The earliest phase lasted from the foundation of Rome until the end of the second century BC. During this period, which saw the demise of the kings of Rome and the establishment of the Republic, the army was comprised of citizens who would join up for a campaign and then return to their families and resume their normal activities.

This had proved a satisfactory way to operate. However, it was also the way in which many of Rome's enemies had staffed their armies during the early days of Rome. As a result, Rome found itself up against armies of a similar quality and consequently Rome was not always successful in battle. Most wars were won eventually but often after initial setbacks and defeats.

There were a number of problems with this concept of a citizen army. Firstly, troops would be loath to spend a long time away from home and would be wanting to get back to their normal day-to-day lives and their families as soon as any battle was over.[2] Another significant problem was that the troops would not have had anywhere near enough time for proper training. Furthermore, those joining the army were required to have a property qualification which meant that only the wealthier could join and the poorer Romans, who formed the majority of the population, were not available to fight.

This situation reached a crisis at the end of the 2nd century BC when Gaius Marius, a consul and general of the army, found he could not recruit sufficient forces and decided to reorganise the army. He abolished the need for a property qualification for service and opened up recruitment to the army to any Roman citizen. In the process, he established a professional army, one whose troops would be paid and who would be provided with all they needed to fight. Marius later married Julia, who was the sister of Julius Caesar's father and was therefore his uncle by marriage.

The reorganised army proved popular with the poorer Romans and the unemployed as they could join up and be clothed and fed. In establishing a professional army Marius stipulated that those serving would be required to do so for a minimum of six consecutive years and for ten more years thereafter. However, at the end of their service in the army, they would be allocated a piece of land by their commander which they could work to provide them with a form of pension.

The way in which the new professional army was structured resulted in a high degree of loyalty to an individual legion's commander. In time, it ultimately evolved into a situation whereby the troops were primarily fighting for their commander rather than the state.[3] The result of this was to fuel the opportunity for the civil wars fought between rival generals during the first century.

With so many new troops and many from a poorer background, with no knowledge of army service, Marius recruited gladiators to train his new soldiers.

For the first time, Rome had a permanent army.

The advent of this new, well trained professional army, occurred at a time when most of the states which had had comparable armies had by then been conquered by Rome. The armies which Rome would encounter in the future would generally have been put together with little or no training as and when they were needed.

This meant that Rome, with a sophisticated, highly trained professional army facing untrained enemies, was entering a period when it was virtually invincible and consequently the first century BC represented a golden age for the expansion of the empire.

The first century BC was also Caesar's century, when he reached the pinnacle of his successes.

This can be called the second phase in the development of the Roman army and the third phase was the development of the army under the emperors, after Caesar. The Roman army under the emperors spent much of the time holding together the existing empire, although some further conquests were made. However, despite a number of successes, Rome was never quite as invincible again as it had been during the first century BC.

Each legion of the army in the first century BC would have had in addition,120 cavalry. The cavalry was usually recruited from local tribes which had been conquered by the Romans and this was an efficient arrangement as it ensured that all the needs of the cavalry, such as fresh horses, fodder etc. could be sourced locally.

In addition, a number of slaves would travel with the legion to assist the legionaries and also any number of auxiliary troops from conquered territories. Those auxiliary troops were normally rewarded after their service with Roman citizenship.

The numerical structure of a legion at the time Caesar invaded Britain would have comprised ten cohorts, nine of which would have consisted of six centuries of 80 men, and a 1st cohort which was made up of five double centuries of 160 men. This made a total of 5,120 legionaries, plus, of course, the cavalry, slaves and auxiliaries.

Supplying the needs of so many men was a formidable challenge. It is a truism that the overwhelming secret to military success is a sophisticated system of logistics. There needs to be a constant supply of food for the troops, fodder for the horses and other animals and adequate backup supplies of arms and equipment.

Vegetius, writing in the late fourth century AD, stated that the main principal point in war was to secure plenty of supplies and to weaken or destroy the enemy by famine.[4] It is self-evident that if troops don't eat they cannot fight. Similarly, support animals will need food to ensure they have the strength to carry their loads.

The Roman army was supplied in a number of different ways. By the first century BC, sophisticated supply chains were available to bring food and arms to the army in the field from various parts of the Roman empire. In addition, a large Roman army would establish supply dumps along the line of its marches with baggage trains continually going back and forth collecting supplies for the men in the field. This arrangement would need troops to be stationed along the supply lines to protect the baggage train and it is most likely that it was this arrangement that Caesar used on his march from the coast to Cassivellaunus' camp at Wheathampstead.

The bigger the baggage train, the more vulnerable it would be. For a large army, the baggage train would stretch back many miles along the route of the march and therefore it was always preferable to establish a continuous supply chain serviced from supply dumps.

Nonetheless, out of necessity, a large quantity of supplies would still need to be carried with the army on the march in a baggage train, normally at the rear of the marching army. The baggage train would also carry the troop's personal possessions. The rearguard to protect the baggage train from attack would consist of a legion or a number of cohorts and this was usually made up from the less-experienced legionaries.

Each man would carry rations to last for a day or two in addition to his weapons and equipment. All this baggage would be carried by a legionary in his *sarcina* or marching pack, which was carried on a forked stick called a *furca*.

Many different types of animals needed to be fed, including mules who would carry light loads at a reasonable speed and oxen which were very slow but could haul wagons with heavy loads. The cavalry horses needed fodder and all-in-all for a legion, the demands of food for its animals was massive. Whenever possible, animals were put out to graze but unless there was adequate grazing available locally and the time to ensure that the animals were fully fed, much of the feed would have to be brought in the baggage train.

The baggage necessary for an army, in addition to food and fodder, would include tents, clothing, weapons, bridge-building equipment, timber and even a field hospital with medical staff for attending to the wounded.

By far and away the most efficient means of supplying the army would be by river transport and whenever possible this would be used as the preferred option, particularly when vast amounts of grain, hay and other animal fodder were required.

The sophisticated methods of supply employed by the Roman army gave it a massive advantage over its enemies and was as significant in winning victories as the prowess of the fighting legionaries.

The food supplied to the legionaries, and often carried by them on the march, was primarily grain which they would grind into flour and cook on portable wood-fired ovens. There was no such thing as a catering corps in the Roman army. Each man fended for himself or a group of men would prepare food together. The legionaries did eat meat when it was available, and this would mainly be either beef or pork. It is interesting to note that when Caesar conquered the Catuvellauni camp at Wheathampstead, he captured a number of cattle. The army would have fed well that night.

Each legion had a standard, comprising a silver eagle on a pole. Although intended initially to be a rallying point in battle, these came to be revered as almost religious symbols and when a marching camp was being prepared, the standards were planted in the ground. Once the camp had been set up, the standard would be kept in a shrine and guarded day and night.[5]

Temporary marching camps were secure areas and would have been almost impossible for an enemy to take. The camp would include a hospital for attending to any wounded and would often be where a supply dump was kept.

Marching camps were constructed in a square or rectangular shape and surrounded by a ditch. These would be dug by legionaries who carried an entrenching tool for the purpose. Each man was allotted a short stretch of the ditch to dig himself and the whole exercise would be completed in a very short time. Whilst this was being done, the cavalry and any legionaries who had not been allotted entrenching duties, would guard those who were completing the defensive ditches.

For obvious reasons, whenever possible, marching camps would be sited close to a source of water.

The march itself could take many hours, not that the legionaries marched slowly, but that simply with so many men, as well as auxiliaries, slaves, and the baggage trains, the whole march would stretch for many miles.

The legionaries would be at the head of the march and they would begin constructing the marching camp whilst the rest of the column was catching up with them. Normally, experienced legionaries would lead the march with the least experienced making up the rearguard to protect the baggage train.

The legionaries marched six abreast and therefore it is easy to see that with over 5,000 men in a legion, the column would stretch back a very long way – easily at least a mile.[6] It has been estimated that a whole army could take six or seven hours to complete a march from camp to camp as the speed of the baggage train would dictate the overall speed of the marching column. The marching column would be headed with the trumpets and standards of the legions.

Although the march of a large army could be a long and occasionally slow process, in the right circumstances, an individual could travel long distances in a short time. It is said that Caesar once travelled by carriage 100 miles a day for eight days in succession.[7]

When it came to fighting, the Romans preferred to operate on the basis of a pitched battle with troops formed up in a regular pattern, although when necessary, the legionaries were perfectly capable of fighting against an enemy operating guerrilla tactics, as indeed did happen on a number of occasions during Caesar's invasions of Britain.

The optimum size of an army fighting a pitched battle was two legions which, with auxiliaries and cavalry, would total well in excess of 10,000 men. Later, under the emperors, more than two legions would sometimes be fielded but in the later years of the Roman Empire, the size of a legion was often much smaller than it had been in the first century BC.

Before, a battle, the commander would address the troops to whip up their fighting spirit, emphasising their esprit de corps. The line-up for a battle would consist of a left wing, a centre and a right wing.[8] The right wing would include the 1st cohort, and the commander would generally position himself on that right wing. The commander usually wore a scarlet cloak, as did Caesar, so that he could be readily recognised by his men.

The commander would not usually fight personally but would travel through the ranks in order to assess how the battle was going and to give orders. Instructions and orders were communicated by bugle calls[9] and a sophisticated system of calls existed which would be learned carefully by each legionary and regularly rehearsed.

In skirmishes, and sometimes in battle, the legionaries would form a tight square and lock their shields around them and over their heads, providing complete protection from enemy blows. This was known as the *testudo* which translates as 'tortoise' so named in view of the way it looked when complete and especially when the legionaries began to advance in that formation.

Whenever possible, the Roman army would form up on high ground to give them a tactical advantage. This did not always work out in cases of surprise attack, as happened when Caesar's foraging party was suddenly attacked by the British during the second campaign in 54 BC, as it was the enemy who swooped down from the hills on all sides to attack the legions. Nevertheless, on this occasion, the Romans once again prevailed.

Life for the ordinary Roman soldier was disciplined, orderly but also often harsh. Discipline was imposed at all times and the punishment for infractions could be very severe. These included being beaten. For severe misdemeanours, a man could be clubbed to death or even crucified.

The Romans practised a process of decimation which would be used in the case of mutiny or desertion. Groups of ten men would draw lots and the one who lost would be killed by the other nine often by clubbing or stoning to death. Those who were left would then be put on a diet of barley rather than the normal wheat and this was intended as a humiliation as barley was regarded as food for animals.

The reasoning behind the practice of decimation was that the Romans believed that soldiers should behave as one and that any fault of one was the fault of them all. They couldn't kill all the culprits as they would then have no army left, so decimation was used as a form of collective punishment and a deterrent for the future.

Following the reforms of the army by Marius at the end of the second century BC, many of the poor in Rome saw the army as an attractive proposition since they would be paid, clothed, fed and also provided with their weaponry. Prior to the reforms, when Rome relied on a citizen army, the individual soldiers had had to provide their own weapons.

In particular, soldiers in the new professional army were paid. Caesar paid his soldiers 900 sestertii per annum although the sestertius would be the equivalent of less than £1 in today's money based on its silver content. However, Roman soldiers were stopped the cost of their food and clothing out of their pay and the result was that they were generally left with little or no money.

Although the Roman army held great store by regular training, the Roman soldier would often take many years to reach the peak of his fighting efficiency. The Centurions who were in charge of a century of eighty men, were chosen on merit for their particular abilities. Early training for Roman soldiers would involve, amongst other activities, perfecting stone throwing and both cavalry and infantry would also train by marching twenty miles in a day.

The main weapons of the Roman soldier were the sword known as a *gladius,* a javelin, called a *pilum,* slings and the bow and arrow, although it has been said that Caesar very rarely used archers. Larger weapons, particularly for siege warfare included the *ballista*, which was a structure for hurling very large stones and boulders, the strings for which were made from horse hair and on a few occasions, women's hair.[10]

In addition to his *pilum* and *gladius* each legionary would also carry a pack of sling shot which would be either small lead balls or small round stones which they gathered when available. The sling shot might not be sufficient to kill a man, but it could knock him out, thus allowing the legionary to execute the *coup de grace*. In battle, the legionary wore chain mail and a helmet, and he carried a shield.

Later in the first century BC, and certainly by the time Caesar was campaigning in Gaul, legionaries were being trained to carry out other tasks as well as fighting. Some would be trained as boatbuilders and repairers, others as engineers, and also clerks and veterinary surgeons.[11] They remained first and foremost fighting men, but their additional skills enabled the legions to be almost self-sufficient.

Chapter Five

The Invasion of Gaul

There are a number of theories as to why Caesar embarked on the Gallic campaigns which ultimately culminated in the conquest of the whole of Gaul. A popular theory is that he was deeply in debt and needed to conquer Gaul in order to gain enough plunder to pay off his creditors and then to keep him in luxury. Another view is that Caesar embarked on the campaigns in order to achieve glory and to place himself in a position whereby he could become the most powerful man in Rome.

Both of these happened as a result of the Gallic campaigns, but the real reason for them was probably much simpler and that is that the conquest of Gaul started more by accident than design, although it became increasingly clear to Caesar that if he did not gain control over Gaul, the danger was that the German tribes would conquer it and then prove to be a continuous threat to Rome.

Caesar's own account of the conquest comprises seven books with an eighth written by his friend and colleague, the consul Aulus Hirtius. Each book covers roughly one year of campaigning.

Book 1 opens with the famous statement that all Gaul is divided into three parts, although arguably there were five. The three parts were Belgica, Aquitania, and the central part called Celtica which were still independent tribal lands. In addition, there was Cisalpine Gaul and Transalpine Gaul which had been part of the Roman empire for some time.

Caesar was initially appointed as governor of Cisalpine Gaul but, soon after his appointment, the governor of Transalpine Gaul died, and Caesar became governor of both provinces. He may well have only remained as governor of these two provinces had it not been for action taken by a neighbouring tribe, the Helvetii who inhabited part of modern-day Switzerland. The Helvetii felt hemmed in and wanted to move their entire population to the west coast of Gaul but in order to do so they would have to travel either by a pass in the north, which would take them through the territory of the Sequani who were allies of Rome, or south through Transalpine Gaul, a Roman province.

The Helvetii took the line of least resistance and marched north through the land of the Sequani and on through the land of another tribe, the Aedui, who were long term allies of Rome and also the Ambarri. The Helvetii plundered the land they passed through and as a consequence, the Aedui and Ambarri turned to Rome for assistance.

Caesar agreed to help, particularly as the Helvetii had defeated a Roman army fifty years before and he was keen to get revenge and he did, by defeating the Helvetii. He then sent them back to their homeland as he was concerned not to leave the area unoccupied in case the German tribes marched in and became neighbours of Rome on the borders of Transalpine Gaul.

A leading German, Ariovistus, who had lived in Gaul for some time, having moved there as a mercenary to assist in fighting against the Aedui in inter-tribal wars earlier, was keen to open up the country to more German immigration. German land was nowhere near as fertile as Gaul and the plan was to remove all the Gauls and settle the land instead with people from Germany – an early plan for ethnic cleansing. Caesar was concerned that if the Germans were to conquer Gaul, then the next step would be that they would invade Italy and Rome would be under threat.

Caesar met with Ariovistus under a white flag but found that Ariovistus was arrogant and boasted that whereas Cisalpine and Transalpine Gaul were Roman territory, the rest of Gaul was for the Germans and that Caesar should get off his land. He had the opinion that he was Caesar's equal. Eventually there was a showdown and a battle was fought near the Rhine at which Caesar was successful and Ariovistus fled across the Rhine.

The following year, it was the turn of the Belgic tribes to rebel. These tribes occupied the part of Gaul which corresponds with modern Belgium and the southern Netherlands. They were concerned that they would be next if the Romans conquered the whole of central Gaul.

The Belgae had originated in Germany and had occupied northern Gaul having expelled the previous inhabitants of the area. Although they were strong and reputed to be very brave, the Belgae were roundly defeated by the Roman armies. They fled back to their villages and the Romans chased after them and killed a great many of their number.

Caesar then carried out a process of picking off each tribe of the Belgae one by one. The tribes were frightened at the sight of the ballistas and other siege equipment and progressively Caesar was able to subdue each tribe and eventually all of the Belgae surrendered.

Caesar then embarked on a process of clemency which he would eventually roll out throughout Gaul. He forgave the Belgae for their rebellion against him and restored them to their lands, albeit as client tribes of the Romans. One tribe, however, the Atuatuci, despite having been a recipient of Caesar's clemency and having indicated that they would obey him, attacked the Roman army. Caesar defeated them and as a reprisal, he had the whole population of the tribe, 53,000 people, sold into slavery.

Finally, Caesar had subdued the tribes of the Belgae and they promised to obey him in future and to send the usual hostages to make sure they kept to their side of the bargain.

For a while there was peace throughout Gaul and as a result of Caesar's successes, Rome declared a public thanksgiving to Caesar of fifteen days; longer than anyone had been previously granted.

While Caesar was back in Rome, one of his legions had been quartered for the winter in modern day Switzerland. While the Romans were preparing their camp and laying down a stock of grain for the winter, they spotted the local tribe on the hills around them preparing to run down and rain javelins on their camp. The local tribesmen were from the Veragri tribe and were far more numerous than the Roman legion. Nevertheless, the Romans defeated the far superior enemy and afterwards the local commander of the legion, Galba, set light to the local villages and withdrew to safer territory.

The next rebellion in Gaul came from the entirely opposite side of the territory, from the Veneti who were a seafaring tribe from south Brittany. The Veneti started whipping up support from other local tribes and, most interestingly, gained help and support from tribes in Britain.[1]

The Veneti presented a problem from an army's point of view in that most of its camps and villages were on the coast and consequently there was only one way to attack them, which was from the landward side which was always heavily defended. Caesar came to the conclusion that the only way to defeat the Veneti would be to do so at sea. He therefore had a fleet of ships constructed and set sail to attack the Veneti fleet.

The Romans had little experience of fighting at sea and, in any case, the Veneti's ships were superior to those of the Romans. Nevertheless, the Romans worked out a method to disable the rigging on the Veneti ships rendering them unable to move. It was then a simple matter of attaching grappling hooks to the enemy ships, hauling them towards the Roman boats and then attacking the crews just as they would have in a land battle. The Roman fleet defeated the Veneti and they surrendered.

Meanwhile, whilst Caesar was fighting the Veneti. Aquitania in south-east Gaul was conquered by one of Caesar's subordinate generals, Publius Crassus, the son of Marcus Licinius Crassus who had earlier formed the triumvirate with Caesar and Pompey.

Towards the end of the year, Caesar marched against the two Belgic tribes, the Morini and the Menapii. Although Belgica had been defeated, these two tribes had remained armed and therefore represented a potential threat to Rome. Caesar attacked them, but it proved to be a somewhat indecisive campaign.

Early in 55 BC, two German tribes, the Usipetes and the Tencteri, had crossed the Rhine into Gaul to escape from a third German tribe, the Suebi, who had been attacking them and preventing them from growing their crops. As a result, Caesar marched through Belgae to meet with representatives of the two tribes but when he met up with them they told him that they didn't want to fight the Romans and if Caesar would give them some land then they would live peaceably but if not, they would have to resort to force. Caesar told them that he hadn't got any land to give them. They parted from Caesar, bragging that they could conquer almost any army.

Caesar decided to march his army towards the two German tribes. The Romans engaged them in battle and overcame them and the Germans withdrew back to the Rhine where they tried to cross but many of them were drowned. Caesar then decided to cross the Rhine and quell any further possibility of action by the German tribes.

The local Gallic tribes offered Caesar boats to cross the Rhine but he declined their offer on the grounds that boats were too risky and also because he felt that to travel across by boat was beneath his dignity. Instead he decided to build a bridge which he completed in only ten days.[2]

Caesar stayed in Germany for a few days, burning villages and farms and stealing crops. He planned to go after the Suebi but decided against doing so as little would be achieved by defeating them as he clearly did not intend to conquer any territory beyond the Rhine and he felt that his mere presence east of the Rhine was enough to deter any further invasions of Gaul by the Germans. Having achieved his objectives, Caesar crossed back over the Rhine into Gaul and destroyed the bridge so that he couldn't be pursued.

Next came the two invasions of Britain in 55 BC and 54 BC which are dealt with in detail in later chapters. On his return from Britain in 54 BC, Caesar spread his legions throughout Gaul in the manner of an army of occupation.

The harvest in Gaul in 54 BC had been poor and, despite this, the Romans were still demanding grain from the local tribes. The Belgic tribes understandably resisted this plundering of their food and having engaged a large force of German mercenaries from across the Rhine to join up with them, the Eburones and other Belgic tribes began a rebellion against the Romans under their leader, the Eburones king, Ambiorix.

The rebellion started when a few Roman troops out foraging from the legion, wintering nearby were attacked and killed. Ambiorix then sent a message to the legionary commanders telling them that the local tribes were about to attack and that the German mercenaries were on their way. In order to trick the Romans, he said he had not approved of the planned attack and that if the legion wanted to withdraw from their camp to safer territory, he would ensure safe passage for them.

51

Despite the fact that it was well established that a Roman legion was far safer from attack within its camp, the two commanders, Sabinus and Cotta fell for Ambiorix's trick and duly left the camp. Then on the road, the legion was attacked and most of the troops killed. Sabinus in particular made a hash of the battle and ended up surrendering to Ambiorix who despite promising he would treat the Romans fairly, massacred the prisoners he had taken. Some legionaries managed to escape capture and returned to the camp but the Gauls attacked the camp relentlessly and as the occupying troops decided that death would be preferable to capture by the Gauls, they committed suicide. A few did however manage to escape and bring the news of the loss of the legion to Labienus.'

When he heard the news, Caesar was furious. The Romans had suffered an unprecedented and humiliating defeat and a complete legion plus five additional cohorts had been wiped out.

The Belgae then attacked another legionary camp which this time held out until Caesar was able to arrive with his forces. Finally, the Belgae were defeated and Caesar set about picking off all the tribes which had joined with Ambiorix one by one. Eventually all the tribes surrendered and Ambiorix crossed the Rhine into Germany to escape.

After this, a rebellion by the Treveri tribe based near the Rhine south of Belgica, led by its chief, Indutiomarus, was put down by Caesar's second-in-command Labienus, and Indutiomarus was killed.

Caesar decided he would cross the Rhine a second time, partly in order to punish the German mercenaries who had come to the help the Treveri and the Belgae, but also to ensure that Ambiorix would not be able to seek asylum there. He learnt that the Suebi, the largest and most powerful tribe in Germany and the tribe who had provided the mercenaries, had retreated to the other side of Germany. Concerned not to stretch his supply chain, he decided against pursuing them and he re-crossed the Rhine back into Gaul. He only partially dismantled his bridge over the Rhine so that it would remain as a lasting reminder to the Germans that he could come and attack them whenever he wished.

Arriving back in Gaul, Caesar set about hunting down Ambiorix. Although he often heard that Ambiorix was nearby he never succeeded in finding him and Ambiorix managed to evade capture. He crossed the Rhine to Germany and was never seen again.

Caesar was so angry that he laid waste to all the Belgic lands and wiped the Belgic tribe the Eburones off the face of the earth in a fit of genocide. His anger was partly motivated by the disapproval of the senate in Rome at the loss of so many Roman soldiers and the stigma that such a loss left.

Once again, Gaul seemed to have been successfully conquered and all was quiet. However, in the south, the leader of the tribe of the Averni, one Vercingetorix, was planning a revolt and this would turn out to be the final decider between the Gauls retaining their independence and rule by the Romans.

The catalyst for the revolt was the news that Rome appeared to be in turmoil following the assassination in January 52 BC of one of its most influential politicians, a consul, Publius Clodius Pulcher. The Gauls were convinced that this would mean that Caesar would need to return to Rome and would then have had his eye off the ball as far as Gaul was concerned. They could not have been more wrong.

Caesar got to hear of what was happening whilst he was in Italy and despite it being the middle of winter decided he had better get back to Gaul as soon as possible. He joined up with his troops stationed in the country of the Helvetii tribe and he crossed the Cevenne mountains in south central Gaul, which the Gauls thought were impassable in winter, and entered the land of the Averni. The Averni were wrong-footed by Caesar's crossing of the Cevennes and were terrified that the Romans would exact violent revenge.

Vercingetorix had, meanwhile, enlisted a number of tribes, all of whom had unanimously voted him King of Gaul. At the time of Caesar's crossing of the Cevennes, Vercingetorix was in central Gaul north of the Averni lands and he quickly marched south to confront the Roman army.

One of Vercingetorix's closest tribes massacred Roman merchants and a number of Roman troops who had established themselves in the town of Cenabum, modern day Orleans. Caesar put the town under siege but most of the enemy left the town quietly by night.

In his fight against the Romans, Vercingetorix used many of the tactics which Caesar used. For example, he operated a scorched-earth policy despite the fact that the land was that of his allies, even burning down whole towns so as to deny them to the Romans. The citizens of one town however, Avaricum, near the modern-day city of Bourges in the centre of France, convinced Vercingetorix that it was impregnable and therefore should not be razed. He allowed it to remain untouched but, as a result, Caesar besieged it and it eventually fell to him.

In order to take revenge for the killings at Cenabum the Romans decided that rather than enslave the population of Avaricum, they would kill them all and slightly less than 40,000 Gauls were massacred as a result.

The next encounter was at the town of Gergovia, the capital of the Averni tribe. The Romans were laying siege to the town when the forces of Vercingetorix swooped down on the Roman troops from higher ground and forced Caesar to retreat, resulting in a battle won by Vercingetorix. This latest campaign was proving to be much more difficult for Caesar.

The Aedui, a tribe which had always been loyal to Rome, now seemed to have sensed blood and began to plot against the Romans. Caesar had trusted them to the extent that he had stored virtually everything he had in an Aeduan town called Noviodunum on the Loire, including his hostages, his grain stores, his money and his private goods, as well as those of his troops. The Gauls then plundered the town and took as much grain as they could and the rest they threw into the river. They massacred the merchants who lived there and burnt the town and the surrounding area to ensure that there would be nothing left for the Roman armies.

Caesar rushed to Noviodunum as fast as possible, the army crossing the Loire at a ford. but it was too late.

The situation had now developed into a full-scale revolt in Gaul with all the tribes involved, with the exception of two who remained loyal to Rome, the Remi and the Lingones and a third, the Treveri who remained neutral.

In a piece of irony, Caesar sent a message across the Rhine to German tribes he had defeated in the past to send across cavalry and some infantry to supplement his numbers. Meanwhile

Vercingetorix was telling his troops that all they needed to do was to prevent the Romans from gaining any food from the land and they would be free men again. 'The hour of victory is come,' he said.

Vercingetorix marched his troops to Alesia in north-central Gaul where he holed up in the town. He was followed there by Caesar who then laid siege to the town.

Meanwhile, Vercingetorix convened a council of all the Gallic tribes and dictated how many additional troops each tribe should contribute to his armies. Present at this council was Commius, who had previously been made chief of the Morini tribe by Caesar, and who had helped Caesar in his invasion of Britain but was now conspiring against him. It is probable that Commius was a traitor to Caesar all along and may well have been the source of the information to the British that resulted in the supposedly compliant British tribes lining up along the cliffs of Kent and attacking the landing in 55 BC, and fighting the battles in Kent after the second landing in 54 BC.

The Gauls under siege by the Romans at Alesia were running out of food but those Gauls who were outside the town spotted a gap in the Roman's siege works and attacked. In the battle that ensued, the Romans won decisively and the Gauls surrendered. Vercingetorix surrendered personally to Caesar and was held captive in Rome for five years. The other Gauls who had fought were given as slaves to Caesar's troops with the exception of Aeduan and Arvernian troops which Caesar kept in order to try to influence their tribes to rally once again behind Rome.

The Battle of Alesia was the last major battle in Gaul and apart from some further minor rebellions, Gaul was now firmly part of the Roman Empire.

This time, Rome declared twenty days of thanksgiving.

Those final rebellions following the battle of Alesia saw a major change in Caesar with regard to the tribes who had rebelled. He started using a process of forgiveness or clemency to defeated tribes. No doubt this was a deliberate policy to get tribes on his side and thereby to hold together the new empire of Gaul. The tribes who were defeated no doubt knew of how vicious Caesar could be in victory and would therefore have really respected the fact that they had retained their land and their lives.

The pattern of behaviour of the Gauls changed in that any subsequent fighting was internecine between tribes and the Romans tended to act as an occupation army, policing any infractions.

Commius continued with his treachery, which must have been deep-seated within him, and no doubt he had been a sort of double agent for many years. Caesar's second-in-command, Labienus, was determined to track Commius down but failed to do so. Commius escaped to Britain where he became King of the British Atrebates, whose capital was at what would later become the Roman town of Calleva Atrebatum or modern day Silchester.

The last significant operation against a Gallic tribe was at Uxellodunum in the Dordogne, where the Gauls were holed up in the town and were besieged by the Romans. The siege was won because the Romans were able to cut off the water supply to the town and the inhabitants eventually had to surrender. Although Caesar was now following a policy of clemency to former enemies, he felt he had to make an example at Uxellodunum, if only to make sure no other tribes decided to rebel. Everyone who had borne arms against the Romans at Uxellodunum had their hands cut off.

Gaul was now thoroughly subdued and conquered. Caesar carried out no further punishments and indeed gave rich presents to the principal local citizens. The Gauls were thoroughly exhausted by all the fighting and from then on lived in peace under Roman rule.

Caesar had won his greatest victory.

However, that victory came at a heavy price for the Gauls. He is said to have enslaved over a million people by the end of the campaigns and personally he had become a very rich man from all that he had plundered.[3]

Chapter Six

Britain at the time of the invasion

T he popular vision of Britain at the time of Caesar's invasions is of an uncivilised, sparsely populated country, with vast forests and primitive tribesmen. However, this could not be further from the truth.

Much research over the years, together with the results of archaeological studies, has yielded a picture of a reasonably sophisticated society with good transport networks, societal structures based on law, and an agricultural subsistence both arable and pastoral with farmsteads and associated farm buildings.

Caesar talks of foraging parties to gather grain and he also refers to animal husbandry when he stormed Cassivellaunus' camp at Wheathampstead and purloined his cattle.

Far from living in mud huts, there is evidence that the farmsteads that the Britons lived in were substantial buildings[1] and some within villages[2]. Most would have been built of wood, which explains why little archaeological evidence of these buildings exists today. This is borne out by Caesar's references to the burning of buildings as a reprisal. There is also evidence that the British kept slaves, which was far from unusual as it was a universal practice throughout all societies at the time.

The society was well organised, and the Britons had their own coinage. Control of that society was mainly in the hands of the druids who were a priestly class but seem to have been more concerned with the law and scholarship and with the customs and history of the people rather than with any religion.[3]

It would also seem that wood was the main material that the Britons used to make the roads, without which they would never have managed to drive their chariots from battle site to battle site. There would of course be little present-day evidence of the existence of these roads as the wood would long ago have rotted.[4]

Some theories suggest that these roads established by the Britons were taken over by the Romans after the Claudian conquest, but that is unlikely. The Romans tended to construct their roads in straight lines, only veering from the straight line as they surveyed the roads from high ground to the next high ground on the route. It is also likely that the Britons would have constructed their roads to bypass land owned by individual farms, much as the later Saxons did, which gave us the somewhat winding roads we have today.

G K Chesterton summed it up lyrically in his poem *The Rolling English Road*[5]: 'Before the Roman came to Rye or out to Severn strode, The rolling English drunkard made the rolling English road.'

Trade with the continent of Europe was important to the Britons. As well as the export of grain, there was trade in Cornish tin and many other commodities.

If we now consider the countryside, much of south-east England in Caesar's time was covered in the Wealden Forest which stretched from present day East Sussex to almost the east coast of Kent. However, it did not extend to Dover or to the north downs, and Caesar's marches were well to the north of the Wealden Forest. The land Caesar marched through would have been farmland much as it is today and given the size of the Wealden Forest, the use of that farmland must have been intensive to ensure sufficient food for the local population. The Britons were skilled farmers. They used a sophisticated version of the plough and used manure to fertilize their fields and it is also reported that they used an early version of a harvesting machine.[6]

There were of course hill forts such as Bigbury and Denge Wood but many of these were just fortified villages. Hill forts were used in times of war to provide a secure base from which to defend the population and also to attack the enemy. However, these hill forts were coming to the end of their popular use by the time of Caesar's invasion.

In order to get a perspective on the task facing Caesar, it is necessary to consider the population of England and how many Britons he might have been facing.

Various sources state the population of England around the time of Caesar's invasion as between 1.5 million and 7.5 million people. The incidence of plagues, epidemics and the impact of local internecine wars would have had a vast impact on the actual numbers.

Let us take a midpoint of say 4.5 million in the whole of England. Of these, probably a third would have been children. This would leave 3 million adults of which approximately half would be women. Of the remaining 1.5 million men, maybe roughly 20 percent would be too old to fight, or too infirm or druids, who would not fight, which then leaves 1.2 million men of fighting capability in the whole of England. It's reasonable to assume that the population was fairly evenly spread which means that the number of men of fighting ability in the quarter of the country representing the south east would have been approximately 300,000.

Caesar landed with a vast army totaling roughly 30,000 men. This is equal to 10 per cent of the estimated Britons of fighting age in the whole of the south east, although it is highly unlikely that all of these or anywhere near this total would have been fielded at any one time. We can see therefore that Caesar was perfectly adequately equipped to take on any of the Britons and particularly when we take into account the differing skills between the Roman legionary and the average fighting Briton.

The way of life of the ancient Briton at the time of Caesar would seem have been quite settled. Although they were probably not particularly warlike, they were very brave when fighting as they believed, in their religion, that when they died, their soul would go to another life elsewhere and then be reincarnated back to earth. Death therefore would not hold any fear for them and since the body died but not the soul, they practised cremation.[7]

The ancient Britons invariably practised a form of democracy and elected their leaders. Leadership of a tribe was not necessarily passed down from father to son or indeed daughter.

Although as Caesar says, they wore woad in battle, and they shaved themselves apart from their hair and moustache, they were by no means grubby people. Indeed, they were quite the opposite. At least one commentator states that the Celts invented soap and outside their territory, they were well known for wearing makeup and dressing their hair.[8]

In short, what Caesar would have encountered would have been a fairly sophisticated people living contentedly and understandably concerned to fight to ensure that they should not be conquered by a foreign power.

Chapter Seven

The Invasion of 55 BC

The embarkation ports

Like so much of the mystery surrounding Caesar's invasions of Britain, there have been a number of different suggestions for the port or ports of embarkation from the French coast. In the main, these boil down to two possibilities with perhaps a third. Many people have researched the issue over the years and the consensus had been that the port of embarkation was either Boulogne or Wissant.

Wissant was a thriving port during the medieval period but is not mentioned as such at any time during the first millennium. Nevertheless, the English coast is most clearly seen from Wissant whereas, from Boulogne the English coast is only just visible thirty miles away and usually only at low tide.

Maps were not generally available in Caesar's time. The famous ancient geographer Strabo produced a map of Europe, but it would have been produced after Caesar invaded Britain as Strabo was born in 64 or 63 BC. Nonetheless, there would have been a reasonable consensus at the time of what the mapping geography would be like and Strabo's later map can be considered a fair representation of what was the perceived knowledge of Britain at the time Caesar invaded. Strabo's map shows the west of Britain opposite Wissant and Boulogne and the east coast of Kent is shown as being in the north and, in particular, north of the present-day Calais region. The tides in the Channel might well have been unknown to sailors who only had experience of the Mediterranean and therefore they could have looked across to Britain and felt they could row their Triremes straight across. However, this is not the case, as Caesar

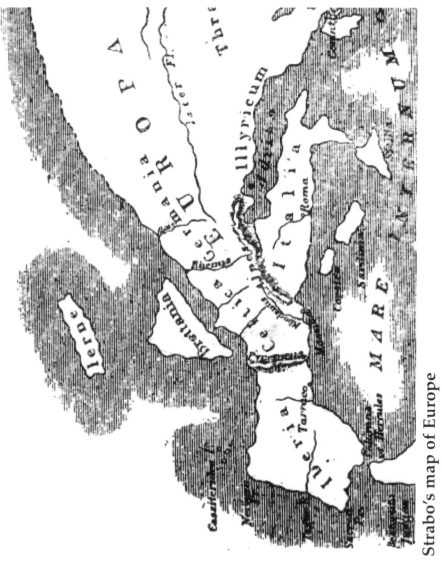

Strabo's map of Europe

would have known, having already sent a warship commanded by Volusenus to reconnoitre the coast of Britain and to look for suitable landing sites. Furthermore, there had been considerable trade between Gaul and Britain and therefore the nature of the passage and the options for harbours on both sides would have been fairly well known.

However, whilst Wissant might possibly have been large enough to accommodate the eighty or so ships which left on the first invasion, ten times that number sailed on the second invasion the following year. Rice Holmes suggests that it would have been impossible to accommodate so many boats at Wissant as it did not have a sufficiently large harbour.[1]

For the second invasion, Caesar had an enormous fleet of ships, 800 or so vessels, including twenty-eight warships and the majority of these were built locally in the intervening year between the first and the second invasion. The materials for fitting them out were to be imported from Spain but wood for the actual construction would have had to have been sourced locally. There is no evidence of woodland around Wissant although Rice Holmes states that this is not the case regarding Boulogne.[2]

Furthermore, Caesar took with him five legions and 2,000 cavalry and left Labienus behind to guard the ports with three legions and a further 2,000 cavalry. If we add the auxiliary troops and other retainers, this is over 50,000 men in total on site[3] and, as any logistician will know, feeding and watering such an army requires a constant supply. There would seem to be no evidence of roads to Wissant pre-dating the later Roman occupation and it would have been impossible to provide for such an army from local fields.

The evidence for Wissant is, therefore, extremely thin and so therefore let us examine the case for Boulogne.[4]

Boulogne is a natural harbour. It would have been such well before Caesar's time and it would have been used by the local tribe, the Morini. However, even Boulogne would not have been able to launch as many as 800 ships (a tremendous number of vessels) at the same time and it is clear from Caesar's own account that the whole fleet sailed as one.[5] One authority even claims that the port of

Boulogne was too small to allow the eighty ships used for the first expedition to be launched together.

Rice Holmes does argue that if the tide was high enough it might have been possible to launch all the ships together, or alternatively they could have been launched in two stages.

Caesar says that Portus Itius was the starting point for the easiest crossing to Britain, a run of about thirty miles. However, the Roman mile was somewhat shorter than our own statute mile and thirty Roman miles would equate to approximately twenty-seven-and-a-half of our modern miles. Interestingly, Folkestone is nearly thirty-four Roman miles from Boulogne but alternatively, thirty Roman miles from Wissant does take you as far as Sandwich in the north and also Lympne in the west.

Another problem faced by the advocates of Boulogne is the question of logistics. The River Boulogne flows eighty-two kilometres from its source but is a small river and it would probably not have had the capacity to bring all the timber needed for ship building. However, there are still forests around Boulogne and therefore the timber might not have needed to be brought a great distance.

Nevertheless, it is questionable whether the River Boulogne could cope with the supply of the food necessary for such a large army of over 50,000 men as well as the fodder for its horses.

Another problem with Boulogne is that by and large it doesn't face Britain. Strabo's map shows it facing the west of the country. In particular, there is the statement made by Caesar himself at the beginning of his account of the first invasion that 'all that coast of Gaul faces north.'[6] However, Boulogne faces west!

So, if there isn't a perfect fit for either Wissant or Boulogne, where did Caesar leave from? An eminent French historian and archaeologist, Albert Grenier, turned his mind to this conundrum back in 1944.[7] The concept of invasions at that time of course was on everybody's minds.

His researches uncovered the fact that in Caesar's time, there was a large lagoon behind a coastal fringe of islands between the modern ports of Calais and Dunkirk. The lagoon is now drained and comprises farmland and a number of drainage ditches. Such a lagoon would have been a perfect place to assemble 800 ships. By carefully analysing Caesar's text, together with the tides and the prevailing weather in that part of France, he reached the conclusion that this was almost certainly Caesar's departure port.

Grenier found that in Caesar's time there was an estuary from the lagoon which stretched all the way inland to what is the modern town of St Omer. This would have opened up the whole of the northern Pas de Calais area for the supply of food, animal fodder and also timber, which would have been in plentiful supply in the region.

The eighteen transports which were allotted to the cavalry during the first invasion were at a point eight miles along the coast. Why not with the main fleet? An answer might well be that with swampy ground around the lagoon; it would have been prudent to keep the cavalry on more solid ground. Interestingly, both modern Calais and modern Dunkirk are each approximately eight Roman miles along the coast from the centre of the area identified by Grenier. Either one could have been the base for the cavalry transports.

Also, the area identified by Grenier is right in the middle of the territory of the Morini and it fits perfectly with Caesar's assertion at the beginning of his account of the first invasion that 'all that coast of Gaul faces north.' Interestingly, Strabo's map shows this to be the case and it also shows the Kent coast as being due north. Although the map post-dates the invasion, it must have been a representation of the prevailing view of the geography at the time.

Almost certainly Grenier has identified the point of departure for Caesar's fleet and incidentally the sea distance of thirty Roman miles takes you to modern day Folkestone to the south and just beyond Deal to the north.

The First Landing

Pin pointing the landing site of the first expedition is extremely difficult, unlike that of the second. The reason is that the information Caesar gives about the landing is open to a number of interpretations.

Caesar writes that he first invaded merely to visit the island, see what its inhabitants were like and also to familiarise himself with the lie of the land, the harbours and the landing places.

Surprisingly, he states that, in general, the Gauls knew nothing about Britain, only the traders who frequently visited the Island.

As a result, he questioned a number of traders to discover what he could about Britain, especially details of the native tribes, their methods of fighting and the harbours capable of accommodating a large fleet of big ships.

In order to acquire more information, he sent one of his tribunes, Gaius Volusenus, to reconnoitre the coast, which he completed over a period of four days. This would have been long enough to enable him to have covered a considerable distance and reconnoitre most of the coast from Thanet round to beyond Hastings.

On the basis that there were almost certainly enough suitable harbours nearer to the French coast, Caesar is unlikely to have been advised by Volusenus to sail as far north as Thanet or round the coast to Hastings or even beyond.

Eighty ships, containing two legions, totalling between 9,000 and 12,000 men, set sail from Portus Itius and a further eighteen ships carrying cavalry left from a point eight miles further along the French coast. This fairly moderate sized force no doubt reflected Caesar's view that having reached an accord with the British leaders prior to sailing he would not meet any opposition to landing. It is this slightly naïve trust on his part which led to the difficulties in the first campaign and undoubtedly caused him to land the following year with an overwhelmingly larger force.

They reached the British coast at around 09.00 hours and found that the enemy had gathered on all the hills, and Caesar writes that he was very concerned because the enemy would be able to hurl javelins on to the narrow beach between the cliffs and the sea.

On the face of it this could refer to a site anywhere between Walmer and Hythe However, given that Volusenus had been charged with finding a suitable landing place and Caesar had questioned traders to try to find harbours capable of accommodating a large fleet of big ships, it is most likely that he was heading for such a harbour. Furthermore, he would almost certainly have set out to cross the channel by the shortest route. So, if we are looking for an existing harbour capable of accommodating a fleet of ships which was closest to the continent then there are three possibilities. These are Dover, Folkestone and possibly Port Lympne which was known to have been a harbour only a few hundred years later during the Romano British era and which had cliffs behind it. We can however discount

Port Lympne as Volusenus would have been unlikely to find it as it would have been too far beyond the undrained Romney Marsh.

As a result of the potential danger from the enemy massed on the cliffs, Caesar anchored off shore and held a conference with his senior officers. He then decided to weigh anchor and as he himself states, proceed a distance of seven miles where he found a landing place and where he then ran his ships aground on what he describes as an open and level shore.

In reality the only two candidates for the port that Caesar anchored off before setting off seven miles along the coast are Folkestone and Dover.

Folkestone was undoubtedly an established port at the time of Caesar. There is evidence that a road led directly from Folkestone to the west of England[8] and this would have been an established trade route.

However, there is a problem with Folkestone being the port from which Caesar's fleet sailed the seven miles to the eventual landing site. Seven miles west of Folkestone are the present-day beaches of the Romney Marsh. In Caesar's time these could not have been the open and level beaches he refers to as behind them was the undrained marsh and he would not have been able to get off the beaches. Seven miles in the other direction is Dover, surrounded by cliffs and therefore he would have again been vulnerable to attack.

Which leaves Dover as the only possibility for the port at which the fleet stood off at anchor and from which it proceeded to the eventual landing place. This conclusion is not new since Dover has been the accepted site for the conference at sea for many years.

All that remains now is to consider which way the fleet went the seven miles to the open and level shore.

Seven Roman miles along the coast to the east is Walmer and seven Roman miles along the coast to the west is Folkestone.

Rice Holmes covers a multitude of pages in his book discussing the prevailing tides and winds at the time of the invasions and comes to the immutable conclusion that because of the winds and the tides, Caesar had to have turned to the north east after discussing with his officers the need to find a safe landing place. His arguments are extremely cogent, but they ignore an article in Archaeologia

Cantiana by a Rev Cardwell writing in 1860[9] who referred to a report by the then Astronomer Royal to the Society of Antiquaries in 1852 stating that Caesar must have travelled westwards.[10] So here we have two completely opposing views.

I'm afraid this demonstrates that the impact of the tides and of the wind direction is a red herring. Certainly, any mariner will have needed to be aware of the tides and the wind direction, but ships are not pieces of driftwood tossed about by the wind and the tides. Roman galleys had oars and other ships had sails, albeit perhaps somewhat primitive sails. Furthermore, given the opinion of the Astronomer Royal in 1852, it is not possible to predict with any accuracy, tides and wind direction on an unknown date 2,000 years earlier. Therefore, from the point at which Caesar consulted with his senior officers, he could have then proceeded seven Roman miles to the east or to the west.

What clues do we have from Caesar himself and also from other sources in antiquity? Caesar talks of an open and level shore. He says that the enemy knew all the shallows, but he gives little more information regarding the coastal terrain.

Dio Cassius, a Roman historian writing over two centuries later, states that in travelling to the landing place from Dover, Caesar rounded a promontory. Valerius Maximus, another Roman historian writing less than 100 years after the event, talks of a rock near the shoreline from which a legionary threw javelins at the enemy.

Anyone looking at a modern map or visiting the two possible landing sites will immediately conclude that it could not be Folkestone because the beach is too narrow. However, we must be aware that the coast has changed considerably in the 2,000 years since Caesar landed.

Also, between Dover and Folkestone there is a promontory at Wear Bay. There is no promontory, however between Dover and Walmer.

Let us then consider the case for Folkestone or Walmer.

On the face of it Folkestone would seem most unlikely as a possible landing place, looking at it today. However, it is well known that it has suffered considerable coastal erosion in the past and that is continuing today, as witnessed by the recent cliff fall at Wear Bay.

Hussey, writing in 1858, refers to the fact that a considerable proportion of the town had been washed away.[11] It is highly possible, therefore, that it had a much wider beach in Caesar's time. Also, before the Leas Area was formed by the massive landslip in 1784, there would have been a much wider beach, exactly as described by Caesar.

Folkestone is known to have been a major port since the Bronze Age and an ancient track way started in Folkestone and led all the way into Wessex.

On the northern outskirts of Folkestone, just above the entrance to the channel tunnel is Castle Hill. This is also known as Caesar's Camp. It was partially excavated by Augustus Pitt Rivers in 1878 who identified it as the site of an eleventh century Norman Castle which had been built over an ancient tumulus which the building of the castle had destroyed. Pottery and iron work were found and Pitt Rivers states that it is possible that some of the iron work could have been ancient. As we shall see later in the book, the tradition of names handed down is a powerful pointer to actual events and the name Caesar's Camp may well refer to somewhere in the vicinity and be misplaced by the passage of time. Alternatively, there may have been a temporary camp under the Norman Castle which has not been found. Castle Hill itself is a massive natural conical hill and if Caesar had landed at Folkestone, there is no doubt he would have used it as a lookout.

As to the rocks mentioned by Valerius Maximus, Folkestone has a number of rocks on its shore and Walmer has the Malms[12] which are exposed at low tide.

Walmer does certainly have an open and level shore. It is a little further than seven Roman miles from the coast at Dover but only marginally. There is a tradition within the town that Caesar landed there and there are large ditches reputed to be part of Caesar's camp by the ruins of the old Walmer Manor built in the twelfth century. The alignment of the ditches are 30 degrees and that coincidentally is the same alignment as the marching camps between the coast and Cassivellaunus' camp as we shall see later. However, its positioning indicates that it could also have been the moat to the manor. There is a problem with Walmer's candidacy in that the rocks known as the Malms would not have been visible at the time of year when

Caesar invaded. Furthermore, it is curious that Caesar makes no mention of the fact that there are the remains of a massive ancient earthwork called the Lynch right on the western edge of the beach at Walmer, stretching from beyond Ringwood to the west. These earthworks are clearly man-made and strangely straight. They face north-west and there is no protection from the seaward side. It looks for all the world like an ancient British fort. Caesar writes that he steered his boats towards the enemy's right flank. Therefore, if the landing was at Walmer he would have steered the boats towards the high ground to the west of Walmer and to the site of the enemy fort on the high ground at the Lynch.

As regards Folkestone, there is evidence that the beach was considerably larger in the past and that much of it has been washed away. There are rocks on the shore that could have been those that the standard bearer of the Tenth legion could have landed on. There is the local tradition of a Caesar's camp.

The main difficulty in choosing between Folkestone and Walmer as the site of the first landing hinges on the fact that all we have to go on is information about the shore. Many changes to the shore will have occurred over 2,000 years and it would be wrong to apply what we see today when assessing where the landings took place. The only information we have about the hinterland is the detail of the skirmish with the Britons during a foraging excursion by the Seventh Legion. However what Caesar writes gives us no clue as to the nature of the topography.

The situation therefore is that unlike the second invasion, where we can now be sure of the site of Caesar's movements in Britain, we cannot be sure of where he landed on the first occasion in 55 BC, but we can at least narrow it down to either Folkestone or Walmer.

Chapter Eight

The Invasion of 54 BC

Finding any evidence on the ground for Caesar's invasion in 54 BC has proved to have been almost impossible in the past. This is largely as a result of a fixation over the site of the crossing of the Thames. Most, if not all, of the commentators in the past have been convinced that the crossing must have been near present-day London.

In my researches, I have found that establishing the site of Caesar's crossing of the Thames is pivotal to finding where his marching camps were, and once I had found the site of the crossing, it proved relatively easy to identify the sites of those various marching camps.

Therefore this section of the book does not continue as would be expected, by identifying the landing place and then demonstrating the topographical evidence for the march to Cassivellaunus camp in sequence, but starts with an examination of the Thames crossing which is the key to finding where the temporary marching camps were and also, by extrapolating the route taken by the army, back to the coast, a strong indication of where the landing took place.

Crossing the Thames

Let us now consider where Caesar's army crossed the Thames. We have a clue in Caesar's own writings on the invasion. He states categorically that the Thames is only fordable at one point and there with difficulty.[1]

This immediately creates a problem since it is not true that the Thames would have been fordable at one point only. The Thames is situated on an alluvial plain and although its hinterland upstream of the tidal reaches would have been marshy, the river would have been fordable in many places and certainly in ancient times, and before the embankments were built in the nineteenth century.

Rice Holmes comes close to stating that Caesar crossed the river at Brentford.[2] This was a very convenient conclusion of course because Brentford is one of only two places on the banks of the Thames in the London area which includes the word 'ford' in its name. The other, Deptford clearly refers to a ford over the river Ravensbourne which joins the Thames at Deptford Creek. There may have been a ford over the Thames at Brentford, but the name Brentford means a ford over the River Brent. The Brent rises near Barnet in North London and flows into the Thames at Brentford. A post-Claudian Roman road ran from Londinium to Calleva Attrebatum (modern day Silchester) across the River Brent at Brentford and would have undoubtedly have forded the Brent – at Brent Ford.

Caesar talks of marching to the Thames. It is worth considering that if he had intended to cross at Brentford, he would have marched *parallel* to the Thames. There is also a strong theory that a ford existed at Westminster downriver from Brentford. Indeed in 1952, a peer, Lord Noel-Buxton, sought to prove the Westminster theory by attempting to walk across the Thames at Westminster Bridge which he tried on 25th March 1952.[3] He didn't succeed in proving the existence of a ford, having to swim a short distance in the centre of the river but it has to be remembered that prior to the building of the embankment in the 1870s, which had the effect of pinching the river, it would have been shallower, and certainly in Caesar's time the hinterland would have been flooded to a significant extent which would have further lowered the height of the river. Furthermore, it was the opinion of the late Mortimer Wheeler that based on Romano-British finds from the banks of the lower Thames, the Thames was fifteen feet lower 2,000 years ago.[4]

It would seem, therefore, that the Thames would probably have been fordable at a number of places around the centre of London and to the west of the City. Therefore, how would this square with Caesar's clear statement that the river was fordable at one point only?

There is an explanation, and that is that Caesar forded the Thames not upstream where modern London is today but in fact

1: The coast of Britain on a clear day which is the view Caesar would no doubt have seen when planning his expedition.

2: This plaque is on the beach between Walmer and Deal and it asserts Walmer's claim to be the landing place for the first invasion in 55BC.

3: Dover from the sea. This is where Caesar rode at anchor after having seen the enemy lined up on the cliffs in 55 BC. It is also the probable site of the landing the following year.

4: The defensive ditch on the western side of the camp at Denge Wood overlooking the River Stour.

5: The defensive ditch on the eastern side of the camp at Denge Wood, looking towards Chartham Downs and Iffin Wood.

6: The Long Barrow known as Julliberrie's Grave where tradition had it that one of Caesar's military tribunes, Quintus Laberius Durus, was buried.

7: A view of Chartham Downs from Iffin Wood. As Caesar wrote, the enemy took up a position on the hills at a distance from the camp and then suddenly swooped down on the legionaries from all sides.

8: Another view of Chartham Downs showing the steepness of the land on the northern side of the valley where the Romans were out foraging and where the battle was fought.

9: The Roman fort at Kemsley. The massive ramparts and the ditch are to some extent obscured by the considerable undergrowth and also possibly may have been enhanced by the construction of Swale Way which runs alongside.

10: Much of the Kemsley fort has been lost to commercial use. In particular, a large electricity substation covers much of the site. This view shows part of the ramparts within the electricity substation site.

11: This is where Caesar crossed the Thames, photographed from the ramparts of the Coalhouse Fort at East Tilbury. In Roman times, there had been a ford here and later, when that had become unusable, it became a ferry crossing.

12: Sadly, nothing now remains of the Roman Camp at East Tilbury as the site has been turned over to gravel extraction. However, the area was extensively excavated in the late 1960s and early 1970s which was known as the Mucking Archaeological Excavation.

13: These ramparts are at Loughton Camp in Epping Forest. Loughton Camp was Caesar's last marching camp before the storming of the Catuvellaunian camp at Wheathampstead.

14: The rampart and ditch at Loughton Camp.

15: The ramparts and ditch at Devil's Dyke which is the local name for the fortifications at the Catuvellaunian camp at Wheathampstead.

16: A sign at the entrance to Devils Dyke at Wheathampstead.

downstream. And downstream, there was only one point where the Thames could be forded and that almost certainly would have been with difficulty, as Caesar writes. Also, Caesar states that the Roman Troops forded the Thames with the water up to their necks. Given the flood plain of the Thames prior to the building of the embankment, and Mortimer Wheeler's assertion that the level of the river was significantly lower 2,000 years ago, it is unlikely that the water would have been so deep up-river. However, a crossing further down river could more likely have resulted in the troops wading across with the water up to their necks.

Research reported in the journal of the Kent Archaeological Society in 1976[5] makes a strong case for a fordable crossing of the Thames at the time of Caesar's invasion at a point some three miles east of Tilbury. This would be consistent with the assertion by Caesar that the river was fordable at one point only. The report states that if there had been a ford in Caesar's time, it might later have been replaced by a ferry. There was indeed a ferry at the site for many centuries and it was the only ferry across the Thames at its lower reaches. A track in Kent leading to where the ferry had been still exists, as does a road in Essex on the other side of the river.

If Caesar did indeed cross the Thames from Kent to Essex, he would then have been immediately next to the territory of the Trinovantes. He states that on his march, presumably after he crossed the Thames, envoys from the Trinovantes arrived and sought Caesar's protection from the Catuvellauni. To ensure that the Trinovantes kept their promise, Caesar demanded forty hostages and grain for his army. If he had crossed at Brentford, this would all have to have been transported through the territory of the Catuvellauni over a long distance and would undoubtedly have been hijacked by them. Other tribes also sent envoys and surrendered to Caesar. This alone provides a further argument for the lower Thames crossing.

Mandubracius, whose father, the king of the Trinovantes had been killed by Cassivellaunus, was travelling with Caesar's task force. He would undoubtedly have known of a ford at East Tilbury as this would have been the main and shortest route to the Kent coast and therefore for travelling to and from the continent.

Looking at the site of the crossing today at East Tilbury, it is hard to see how a man and certainly an army could have waded across because not even their heads would now have been above water. However, there is a reason why Caesar's army could have waded across 2,000 years ago and that is the fact that the land has lowered since then.

Geologists have identified a phenomenon called isostatic rebound, also known as post-glacial rebound.[6]

The weight of all the ice during an ice age tends to depress the earth's crust under that weight, pushing it down. When the ice melts, however, the reverse happens, and the land starts to rise back to its former level. This happened in Britain during the last ice age which peaked around 20,000 years ago and finally melted about 10,000 years ago. In Britain the last ice age was confined to an area north of the Wash and south of that there was no ice deposit. When the ice finally melted, the land north of the Wash started to rise due to the isostatic rebound but the effect on the earth's crust was to act like a see saw and as the land in the north of the country rose, that in the south began to fall. It has been found that, in a number of areas, the sea inundated the land in the south of Britain and there is evidence of prehistoric forests where the Solent is now and also in the tidal area between the land and St Michael's Mount in Cornwall.

The speed at which the land sinks in the south of Britain is very slow. It has been estimated that the rate at which the land is sinking in the south of Britain after the last ice age is 5cm per 100 years. Although this is very little movement, it would work out at a metre over the last 2,000 years which means that the river bed at the lower reaches of the Thames would have been a metre higher at the time of Caesar's invasion. Add to this Mortimer Wheeler's assertion that the Thames was fifteen feet lower 2,000 years ago, we can now see that a fordable crossing could well have existed at East Tilbury in the time of Caesar. Furthermore, it is believed that the ford at East Tilbury existed for a long time after Caesar but that eventually it became unusable and was replaced by a ferry. This would be entirely consistent with the effect of isostatic rebound on the crossing over the years.

Today, there is nothing to see at East Tilbury other than possible evidence of a causeway on the northern side of the crossing.

The temporary marching camps

One aspect of the invasions is universally accepted, and that is that Caesar was marching across country and across the Thames towards Cassivellaunus' camp, which it is generally assumed was at modern day Wheathampstead, the site known today as Devil's Dyke.

Having identified that Caesar most probably forded the Thames at East Tilbury, I drew a straight line on a map from the crossing at East Tilbury to Wheathampstead. Slightly more than halfway along that line, it passes an ancient earthwork in Epping Forest called Loughton Camp. Loughton Camp was excavated in 1881 by General Pitt-Rivers who concluded that it was an Iron Age fort dating from about 500 BC but it is not clear what basis he used to come to this conclusion. It is clearly too rectangular to be an Iron Age fort. It looks just like a temporary marching camp and as we will see is very similar to other camps on the route.

Loughton Camp is twenty-one miles in a straight line from the crossing at East Tilbury and therefore the previous camp must have been at or near the crossing. A reasonable distance for an army to march in one day would be fifteen to twenty statute miles, which would leave adequate time to reconnoitre a suitable site for a camp before darkness fell.

The probability is that there would have been one day's march to the site of a camp followed by, say, two days to construct and fortify that camp before setting out again for the next one. The camps were probably also used as supply dumps on the route from the coast to Wheathampstead.

Between two and three miles north of the East Tilbury crossing, at grid reference TQ673803 there was a camp which had started as a hill fort constructed in the Bronze Age. Excavation of the site found that it had been fortified sometime around the beginning of the first millennium by the Romans and at that time fortification ditches had been constructed. The report of this excavation states that the fortifications may have been constructed during the Claudian invasions of 43 AD. The bronze handle from a first century legionary's helmet had been found at the site. However, in view of its positioning and the pattern emerging of the sites and relative distances of Caesar's marching camps, it is almost certain that this refortification was initially constructed by Caesar's army and may later have been used by Claudius. The refortified camp is described as having been rectangular and ditched as is the camp at Loughton, but the East Tilbury Camp has now been obliterated due to the extraction of gravel from the site.[7] As a result, it is not possible to define its size.

Interestingly, if a line is drawn from the site of this camp to Wheathampstead rather than from the East Tilbury crossing, that line passes through the camp at Loughton.

Continuing the line back into Kent from the East Tilbury crossing to Wheathampstead, at seventeen miles from the crossing is another ancient earthwork just north of Sittingbourne at a place called Kemsley, at grid reference TQ912668. This was a rectangular camp and like the Loughton camp was orientated so that the longest side of the camp faced tangentially to a straight line to Wheathampstead. The site is marked on the ordnance survey map as a settlement and it is now covered by an electricity substation, on the edge of an industrial estate.

Today, to travel in a straight line from Kemsley to the Thames crossing at East Tilbury would require crossing over the estuary of the Medway. However, there is no doubt that the topography would have been considerably different in Caesar's day not least due to the fact that the ground will have sunk in the last 2,000 years as a result of the impact of post-glacial rebound.

Continuing the straight line, joining up all the camps further back into Kent, sixteen miles beyond Kemsley is Denge Wood, at map reference TR090529. Once again, the orientation of the camp in Denge Wood is identical to Loughton and Kemsley; it is rectangular and like the other camps has ditches surrounding it. It is an area of high ground, to the east of the Stour, a mile-and-a-half southwest of the village of Chartham. It shows signs of fortification and evidence of a Roman marching camp of the sort that Caesar would have had constructed.

Denge Wood and the surrounding area is where the first major battles were held with the British and more on this later.

My research has shown that the report of the original Ordnance Surveyor who surveyed the area in the nineteenth century decided that it was the site of a mediaeval cattle pen. As a consequence, he drew it on the map as smaller than it is in reality. Vast ditches surround the site, characteristic of Roman fortifications. The site in Denge Wood almost abuts the River Stour and the geography is consistent with the account by Caesar that the Britons had withdrawn to a river.

Caesar devotes a considerable amount of his account to activities at this camp, and it is clear that he must have spent much longer at this camp than at any of the marching camps between there and Cassivellaunus' stronghold at Wheathampstead. This is clearly evidenced by the extent and size of the ditching surrounding the camp.

There is no doubt that these camps, Denge, Kemsley, East Tilbury and Loughton are the marching camps used by Caesar. The distance between them is between sixteen and twenty miles, the distance an army could comfortably travel in a day and leave enough time to bivouac. What is interesting is that all four camps and Wheathampstead are almost equidistant from each other and all are orientated at 30 degrees to the horizontal.

Denge camp to the Kemsley camp was sixteen miles, from Kemsley camp to the camp at East Tilbury, seventeen miles, from that camp to Loughton camp, twenty miles and from Loughton camp to Wheathampstead seventeen miles. The longest, in South Essex at twenty miles, was on the edge of the friendly territory of the Trinovantes whereas the shortest, in North Kent, was an area where Caesar states that his army was constantly harried by the British.

Although all the camps are roughly the same size, albeit that the camp at East Tilbury near the Thames crossing can no longer be measured, the size of these camps is much smaller than would be expected.

Caesar landed in Britain with five legions. He left ten cohorts, which equates to one legion, at the base camp on the coast and took the remaining four legions with him on the march inland.

Temporary camps to house four legions would have needed to be about four times the size of the ones discovered. As such, they would surely have been discovered before now due to their massive size.

One explanation for this discrepancy is that Caesar left a proportion of his troops at each camp and proceeded with the remainder. This makes excellent sense since he would need to ensure his rear was protected and he would want to leave the camps protected for the return journey after reaching Cassivellaunus' headquarters.

Each camp would have been permanently manned by a number of cohorts leaving probably two full legions to capture Wheathampstead. This was the amount of troops Caesar originally felt he needed to attack Cassivellaunus, when he invaded in 55 BC. He had brought these over in 55 BC under the impression that the local tribes would keep their word not to attack his forces and he would then need only to defeat Cassivellaunus. As we have seen, this had not been the case, but by the time he had crossed the Thames in 54 BC, the local tribes had ceased attacking the Roman army and all that remained was for Caesar to attack and defeat the Catuvellauni at Wheathampstead which he could do with his original estimate of two legions.

The ditches and associated ramparts are typical of the type dug by Roman legionaries, all of whom carried an entrenching tool.

When examining these camps, one issue kept coming up and that was that the camps were not aligned north/south as might be expected but at an angle. Also, the same angle applied to each camp. Why was this the case? Then it suddenly became clear, each of the camps was aligned with its entrances pointing directly towards the route the army had come and the route it was to take. This makes sense since it would enable the guards to watch for attacks. All the camps are oriented in such a way that they present their longest side to the direction the army was going to take but most significantly of all, they are all in a straight line and that line ends at Wheathampstead. There was clearly an established route which Caesar was following, probably guided by Mandubracius of the Trinovantes, and Caesar himself writes that Cassivellaunus hid a short way from the route and then if the Romans strayed from the route, he would attack.

It could be argued that as these camps are all in a straight line from Wheathampstead to the coast, they could in fact be Catuvellauni camps. This is a fair question, but on balance the answer has to be no. Firstly, the camps are rectangular and typical of Roman marching camps. Secondly, it is unlikely that the Catuvellauni would have maintained marching camps in territory other than their own.

However, now what is absolutely fascinating, is that if you draw a line on a map linking all four camps with Wheathampstead, that line is absolutely straight! This is most certainly more than a coincidence.

Track that line back to the coast and it ends at Dover.

Cassivellaunus' Camp

Cassivellaunus camp is known to have been in what is now mid-Hertfordshire and there have generally been two candidates for the site. These are either the large Iron Age site at Wheathampstead or the site of the later Roman Town of Verulamium at modern day St Albans.

We have already seen that the four marching camps identified on the route from the coast to Cassivellaunus' camp line up almost exactly in a straight line. At the north western extremity of that line is Wheathampstead. Verulamium is not on the line and therefore circumstantial evidence points strongly to the conclusion that Cassivellaunus' camp at the time of Caesar's invasion was at Wheathampstead.

The site at Wheathampstead was excavated in 1932 by Sir Mortimer Wheeler but he was unable to reach a conclusion one way or the other as to whether or not it was the capital of the Catuvellauni tribe, although he did state that in his opinion he could find no other claimants to the Catuvellauni camp in Hertfordshire.

Caesar states that during his march, envoys came from the Trinovantes, which he said were the strongest tribe in Britain. Their territory was just to the east of the East Tilbury crossing and therefore once he had crossed the Thames, he was very close to their territory but just inside the territory of the Catuvellauni.

He agreed to protect the Trinovantes from the Catuvellauni who were their enemies, and he learnt from the Trinovantes that he was

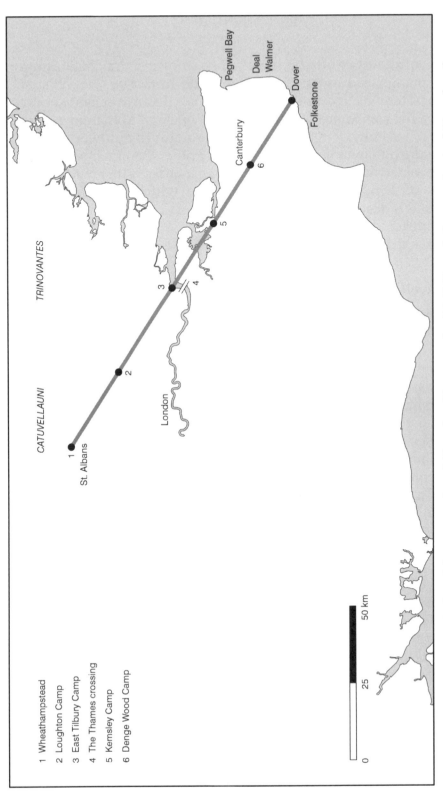

1 Wheathampstead
2 Loughton Camp
3 East Tilbury Camp
4 The Thames crossing
5 Kemsley Camp
6 Denge Wood Camp

CATUVELLAUNI

TRINOVANTES

St. Albans

London

Canterbury

Pegwell Bay

Deal
Walmer

Dover

Folkestone

0   25   50 km

Caesar's route inland in pursuit of Cassivellaunus in 54 BC and the projected line back to the south coast.

not far from Cassivellaunus' stronghold, He therefore continued on the same route, and established his marching camp at Loughton.

It is clear from Caesar's own account that Cassivellaunus was the main troublemaker and that a major reason for Caesar undertaking the invasion was to punish Cassivellaunus and prevent him from making any trouble in the future.

From the Loughton camp, Caesar's army pushed on towards the Catuvellaunian camp which we can now be fairly certain was at Wheathampstead at Map reference TL187131.

We have already seen that Caesar would have left a significant number of troops to guard his marching camps in the rear guard. He set out with four legions, so it might be assumed that by the time he reached the Loughton camp, he would have had between one and two legions to attack the Catuvellauni. Although he needed to protect his rear guard at each of the marching camps, what is clear is that the danger to the Romans came only from Cassivellaunus who whipped up other British tribes and that whilst Caesar had Cassivellaunus on the run, his rear guard would have been fairly safe.

Given the fact that at this stage, the Catuvellauni were unsupported by other British tribes as stated earlier, it is likely that one Legion of 5,000 or so Roman soldiers or certainly two legions of twice that number, would easily have conquered a British tribe's headquarters.

Cassivellaunus' camp was approximately seventeen statute miles from the Loughton camp and therefore given that the army would have marched this distance in less than a day, then Caesar would have reached Cassivellaunus stronghold mid-to-late afternoon. It would seem from Caesar's own account that he marched to the camp and immediately assaulted it, despite the fact that it was well fortified. The Catuvellauni fled precipitously and we can assume that having taken the camp, Caesar then occupied it for his army overnight.

It has been suggested that around 20 BC, the Catuvellauni moved their capital to Verlamion later to be called Verulamium after the Roman conquest and today known as St Albans. It is more likely that the date of 20 BC is too late and that the Catuvellauni would probably have moved their capital shortly after the old capital had been trashed by Caesar.

The final act in this saga is reported by Caesar. He says that while the Roman army was in the Catuvellaunian territory, Cassivellaunus sent instructions to four kings in Kent to attack the Roman naval camp on the coast. This was quickly fought off.

Cassivellaunus then surrendered and agreed to all Caesar's terms, in particular, the provision of hostages and the payment of an annual tribute to Rome.

Denge Wood and the first battle

Up to now, the accepted site for the first encounter and battle with the British has been Bigbury Camp on the western outskirts of present day Canterbury. One of the arguments for this is that it is the only Iron Age camp in Kent. However, a careful reading and analysis of Caesar's own account presents very real reasons to question the assertion that Bigbury was the site.

An argument often advanced in favour of Bigbury is that it is twelve miles from the coast. In fact, it is sixteen to seventeen statute miles from Deal and a similar distance from other candidates for the landing site. This is an entirely spurious argument as the overnight march of twelve miles did not in fact end at the enemy's camp but was the point at which the enemy was first sighted. The enemy then advanced to a river – the Stour[8].

Now what this implies is that initially, the enemy tried to stop Caesar from reaching the river, which is the main reason why it is necessary to discount Bigbury as the site of the British camp because Caesar clearly implies in his account that the skirmish with the enemy was *before* his troops had crossed the Stour, and Bigbury is the other side of the river. However, it is possible that Bigbury could have been the base from which the enemy originally came, and where their wives and families were.

Caesar states that a night march of about twelve miles brought him in sight of the enemy. He probably arrived just before daybreak. He would almost certainly have had a guide who would have led him in the right direction and there must have been existing tracks which could be followed from the coast since they were marching in the dark. The Britons advanced to a river, undoubtedly the Stour, with their cavalry and chariots and tried to bar his way by attacking from a position on higher ground. This demonstrates conclusively that the Britons were holding a position to the east of the Stour and that position was on high ground and situated in a way that would prevent the Romans from crossing the river.

At the northeast end of the site at Denge Wood, there are the remains of defensive ditches and at the north west of the woods, adjacent to the Stour Valley Public footpath, the land slopes steeply down to the river Stour. At the top right-hand corner of the wood is an earthwork.

Sure enough, there are the deep ditches so redolent of a Roman marching camp. The site was on high ground and the Stour was immediately to the west of the site. If the earthwork in Denge Wood was originally an ancient British stronghold; it had been perfectly positioned to prevent any enemy from crossing the river.

There is no doubt that these fortifications which would have been initially created by the Britons, were then captured by Caesar who adapted the fortifications to establish his own camp similar to how he was to do it later at the camp at East Tilbury.

There is further evidence, both substantial, but also anecdotal, to strengthen the claim for this to be the site of the first battle with the Britons.

To the north of the wood is a massive rampart which is likely to be the spoil from the fortification trenches put up as a defence or the remnants of the earlier British defensive ramparts. Various uniformly round small stones can be found all over the site and these are very similar to slingshot stones used by both sides at the time.

There seems never to have been any excavation of the site at Denge Wood, probably because of its reputation as having been a medieval cattle pen! Why a medieval cattle pen should have been constructed with Roman style ditches, is difficult to comprehend.

In short therefore there is overwhelming evidence to suggest that the camp at Denge Wood would have been the first camp established by Caesar after he left the coast on his overnight march.

Also, for both the Britons and later the Romans after they had taken the stronghold, the position was perfect for defence, having the river in the rear.

Caesar writes: 'Being repulsed by our cavalry, they concealed themselves in woods, as they had secured a place admirably fortified by nature and by art, which, as it seemed, they had before prepared on account of a civil war; for all entrances to it were shut up by a great number of felled trees.'[9]

Caesar's troops then locked shields into a testudo and proceeded to capture the stronghold and create a camp for his troops. He says that once he had defeated the enemy, Caesar captured their stronghold, drove them out of the woods and he indicates that he then constructed his camp on the site.

The Britons were seen off and Caesar stopped his troops from pursuing the Britons because he wanted to devote the rest of the day to fortifying his camp.

The Britons waited for a period of time, then while the Roman soldiers were off guard, busy fortifying the camp, the Britons came out of the woods and swooped on the outpost guarding the front of the camp. A violent battle ensued. Caesar himself was not at the camp but out and about and he sent two cohorts to the rescue and despite throwing in more cohorts, the enemy managed to get away.

One of Caesar's tribunes, Quintus Laberius Durus was killed in this battle.

Caesar mentions that on the next day, three legions and all the cavalry were on a foraging expedition beyond the camp and fought a fierce battle with the British cavalry and charioteers but that the Romans won the battle, drove the enemy into the woods and hills and killed many of the Britons, suffering some casualties themselves.

An obvious question is that once Caesar had taken the Britons' camp in Denge Wood, where did the enemy go? Bigbury would have been too far away and would have involved a river crossing in order to attack the Roman camp, besides which the geography is such that there is no space between the river and Bigbury Camp where a battle could have been fought.

So, what about any evidence of the battle between Caesar's forces and the ancient Britons?

There is a candidate for a redoubt that the Britons could have retreated to. Some two and a half miles to the east of the camp in Denge Wood, is an area of woodland called Iffin Wood.

Iffin Wood is about two miles south of Canterbury immediately on the west side of the later Roman road, Stone Street. Within the wood there are a number of earthworks of probably medieval date but also two large Iron Age round barrows and some ancient fortifications. An article in the *Gentlemen's Magazine* of October 1843 by John Yonge Akerman FSA, reports on an archaeological dig by a Matthew Bell at Iffin Wood in January 1842.[10]

Akerman states that the remains of the fortifications at Iffin Wood were supposed by many to be at the place to which the Britons retreated after they were defeated by the Romans. In the wood, there is a tumulus, which is 150 feet in circumference and six feet high. Bell dug a four-foot-wide trench north/south through the tumulus and discovered five large urns irregularly placed. Each urn was placed with the opening face down and was filled with ash, charcoal and minute fragments of bone. If a four-foot-wide trench yielded five large urns with cremation remains in them, the inference must be that the tumulus as a whole contained many more such urns and that therefore the interments were of a considerable number of people. Bell concluded that in view of the apparent haste and irregularity of the interment, the remains were probably those of men killed in battle. Akerman speculated that they might have been the remains of Britons who had died in Caesar's engagement with Cassivellaunus but then dismissed this theory on the basis that Cassivellaunus' stronghold was north of the Thames. The manner of burial and the use of urns was very similar to interments found in other counties and, furthermore, the rite of cremation was commonly practised by Celts within Iron Age Britain.

However, given the proximity of Iffin Wood to Denge Wood and the fact that the ancient Britons practised cremation, it is more than likely that these were the remains of Britons killed in the battle in front of Caesar's camp and that Iffin Wood was where the Britons retired to after Caesar had taken their stronghold at Denge Wood.

The ground between Iffin Wood and Denge Wood slopes sharply from Iffin Wood then flattens out on the approach to the camp at Denge Wood. A perfect place for a battle with the Britons flying down the hill at the beginning to attack the Romans. Indeed, Caesar says that the day after the skirmish at the gates of the camp, the enemy took up position on the hills at a distance from the camp. This can only be Chartham Downs which match exactly the topography Caesar mentions. He says that after conducting guerrilla tactics during the morning, the enemy swept down from all sides. The land between the foot of the Chartham Downs and Denge Wood is ideal for a battle. Caesar says that a great many of the enemy were killed and that they never attacked Caesar again in their full strength.

In addition to the evidence on the ground and that from the positioning of the other camps, there is anecdotal evidence of a more tenuous nature.

Local tradition has it that the long barrow beside the Stour, known as Julliberrie's Grave, was named after the tribune who was killed in the earlier skirmish in front of the camp and that he was buried there. Successive archaeological investigations have failed to find any evidence of an early Roman burial at Julliberrie's Grave although the northern part of the grave was destroyed long ago by chalk diggers. The antiquarian William Camden stated that this was the grave of Quintus Laberius Durus presumably because of a merging of Julius and Laberius. It is now known that the long barrow is Neolithic although there were some later Roman burials found during excavations in the 1930s.

What was found, however, was a hoard of Roman coins. The fact that these were not together but scattered makes one wonder whether or not the later Roman occupiers of Britain were venerating the long barrow with votive offerings and if so why? Local traditions handed down can survive for many centuries and if Quintus Laberius Durus is not buried in Julliberrie's Grave, he could well be interred in one of the tumuli in Denge Wood.

It is clear from Caesar's own account that the army spent quite a long time in this area before it set out for Cassivellaunus stronghold.

On the subject of the passing down of tradition through the ages, W.H. Ireland in his *History of Kent* quotes Camden as having stated that the name of Chilham, the village immediately opposite Denge Wood and on the other side of the Stour, was a corruption of Juliham or Julius' village.[11] Somewhat fanciful but a lovely idea.

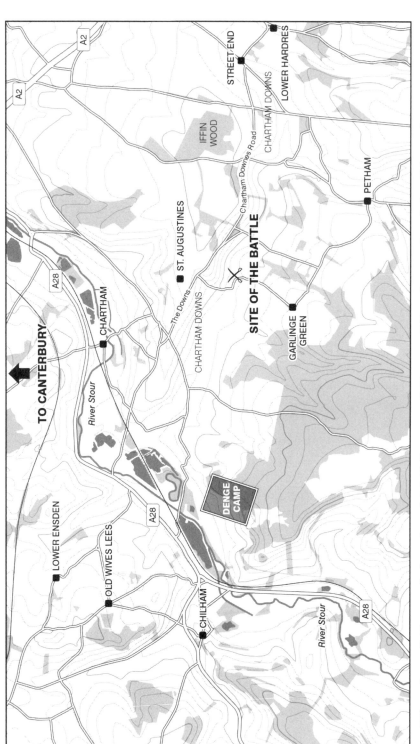

The site of Caesar's battle of 54 BC around Denge Wood, south of the River Stour.

The site of the second landing

Caesar writes that on the second voyage to Britain in 54 BC, when the wind had dropped, the fleet was driven off course by the tides and was leaving the coast of Britain on the port side. Later, the current changed and by dint of hard rowing by all the soldiers, he made the part of the island where he had found the best landing places the year before.

Several commentators have interpreted this account in the past as meaning that he landed at the same place as he had done the year before.[12] However careful reading shows that this is not what he says only that he landed in the part of the island he had landed in the year before.

Caesar would have been well briefed on where the best landing places were by Volusenus who he had sent to reconnoitre the shore before the invasion the previous year. Of the second landing, Caesar says that he disembarked his army and chose a suitable spot for a camp. If he had landed in the same place as he had the year before, he would have simply reused the camp he had prepared on that occasion. This statement by Caesar demonstrates conclusively that the second landing was not at the same place as the first nor close to it.

Recent archaeological excavations on the Isle of Thanet at Pegwell Bay have uncovered a large roman camp with finds dating to the mid first century BC. On the face of it this should be the landing place of Caesar's second invasion in 54 BC.

There is a 'but', however and that is that Thanet is not the only candidate for the landing. Empirical evidence gleaned from field research regarding the various marching camps and the ultimate destination of Wheathampstead, and in particular, the fact that the temporary marching camps and the final destination are all in a straight line, indicate that there is an alternative. It is well known that the mind-set of the Romans was to go straight for their objective. This is exemplified in the Roman roads built later after the Claudian conquest. These generally lead from place to place in a straight line.

Now, the marching camps and the Catuvellauni camp at Wheathampstead happen to be on a straight line, and the obvious question is what happens if you take that straight line between the marching camps and Wheathampstead and track it back to the coast? The answer is that it terminates at what is modern day Dover.

Throughout history, many people have sought to establish where Caesar landed in Britain and the one immutable fact that we should all bear in mind is that it will never be possible to be absolutely certain about anything relating to the Julian invasions.

It is therefore necessary to consider the respective merits and arguments for and against the two candidates for the 54 BC landing, Dover and Pegwell Bay.

First let's consider Dover.

All received wisdom up to now states that Caesar did not land at Dover because the cliffs either side of the harbour would have given an opportunity for the British to hurl their javelins on the Roman army. That was certainly true when the first invasion took place in 55 BC which is why Caesar did not land at Dover on that occasion.

It is highly probable that Caesar was intending to land at Dover on his first expedition and that it was at Dover that the Britons had lined up on the cliffs in 55 BC making such a landing too dangerous. We know that Caesar then travelled seven miles along the coast from Dover to where he eventually landed.

Dover was the main port for trade with the continent in the first century BC and would almost certainly have been high on the list of recommended landing places reported by Volusenus and most probably at the top of that list.

There is nothing inconsistent in Caesar's own writings with his second expedition landing at Dover, but most commentators have misinterpreted his words to assume that since it was too dangerous to land at Dover on the occasion of the first invasion it was therefore equally dangerous to do so on the second. Caesar writes that on the voyage he found that the coast of Britain was fast disappearing off the port side. He was clearly going north-east and therefore he must have turned around, and as he says, the soldiers rowed hard and he made for the part of the island where he had found the best landing places the year before. Undoubtedly, Dover would have been one of the best of those landing places and in fact, Caesar hints at the fact that it was Dover that he landed at by talking of the best landing places and making a point of mentioning that on this occasion the enemy were nowhere to be seen, that they had been frightened by the size of the fleet and taken to the hills. Therefore, why wouldn't he land at the best site finding on this occasion that it was free of the enemy?

Also, he mentions that the fleet was accompanied by privately owned vessels built by individuals for their own use. This use must have been trading or the acquisition of plunder and a port would be the appropriate place to load such booty.

Given that Dover was at the time the main port for trading between Britain and the Continent, if it was left unguarded, it would have been foolish for Caesar to have landed anywhere else.

If Dover was the landing place in 54 BC how does this fit in with the overnight march to encounter the enemy. Most interpretations are that Caesar marched overnight a distance of twelve Roman miles to the first encounter with the enemy at the River Stour. The distance between Dover and the camp at Denge Wood is approximately seventeen and-a-half Roman miles. However what Caesar in fact writes is that he caught site of the enemy after twelve miles of marching and that the enemy then advanced to a river. Twelve Roman miles would have taken him to Iffin Wood in front of which he would have seen the enemy lined up on the hills near the modern hamlet of Petham. Incidentally, a march at night would have to have been over a proven track as otherwise it would be impossible to know where he was going. As has now been established, there was a direct straight-line route between Dover and Wheathampstead, which was probably a route taken by traders to and from the Catuvellauni, and this would have been the route which Caesar took.

Let us now consider the alternative candidate for the landing, the recently-discovered encampment at Pegwell Bay.

The site of the camp is on the Isle of Thanet which was surrounded by the Wantsum Channel prior to a few hundred years ago. This means that the Roman army would have had to cross the Wantsum Channel before starting the overnight march to engage the enemy. It is odd that given the precision with which Caesar writes his account, he did not mention that the army had to cross an estuary at the start of the march. However, there is a possible reason for this and that is that Thanet may not have been an island 2,000 years ago as it too may well have been affected over the years by the impact of isostatic rebound similar to the Thames crossing at East Tilbury and the Wantsum may not have been flooded then.

The dating of the artefacts is pretty compelling evidence, although given the margin of error in carbon dating and generally when attempting to date artefacts accurately, it is quite possible that the site found in the excavations is in fact that of the Claudian landings ninety-seven years later. The site of the Claudian landings has never been found but like Caesar's landings many candidates have been suggested over the years for the site.

If the landing had indeed been at Pegwell Bay, this also fits in with the distance of the overnight march. Iffin Wood and the Hamlet of Petham are also twelve miles from Pegwell Bay.

Caesar states that the fleet was anchored on an open shore of soft sand. The shore at Dover is shingle but equally the shore at Pegwell Bay is a mixture of sand and mud. Who can know what the shore actually consisted of 2,000 years ago?

The landing place is mentioned by Caesar on two further occasions. Having taken the camp at Denge wood, Caesar set out the following day to pursue the enemy whereupon he received a message that the fleet had been badly damaged in a violent storm. He immediately went back to the coast and organised the repair of the damaged ships and in order to prevent any further damage, he ordered all the ships to be beached and enclosed with the camp in one fortification. Alas, it is most unlikely that any remains of these fortifications remain if the landing had been at Dover as the town has been built upon. However, the size of the camp uncovered at Pegwell Bay may well have been large enough to contain the fleet of ships.

Caesar undoubtedly returned to the coast on horseback in order to get there as quickly as possible and took his cavalry with him because he mentions that on the march back to Denge Wood, the cavalry had a fierce battle with the British cavalry and charioteers. However, the Romans won the day.

The second mention of the landing place which Caesar makes is right at the end of the campaign. Although Cassivellaunus had been subdued and his capital sacked, he nevertheless tried one final attack. He ordered four kings based in Kent to attack the Roman naval camp. By then, the Romans were well dug in in a fortified camp and they repelled the attack with no casualties and yet killed very many of the enemy. They also captured one of the kings, Lugotorix. Once Cassivellaunus heard news of the action he realised the game was up and he sent envoys to Caesar to obtain Caesar's terms for a surrender. Those terms were a demand for hostages, an annual tribute to be paid to the government in Rome and an undertaking not to molest Mandubracius or the Trinovantes.

Once the hostages had been delivered, the fleet set sail but in view of the number of hostages the return voyage was made in two stages.

As mentioned above, it may never be possible to say with certainty where the landing in 54 BC took place and therefore the reader will need to make up their own mind. Hopefully, however, if the excavations at Pegwell Bay continue and more finds emerge we will be able to say with much more certainty where the landing took place.

Chapter Nine

Analysis of the conventional view

Over the years, many antiquarians have sought to establish the details of the landing sites and the passage of Caesar through south-east Britain. Those carrying out investigations have included the French Emperor, Napoleon III. Each of the early accounts suggests a number of different sites for the landing but little information about the progress of the campaigns.

Most of these early writings were brought together with a number of additional suggestions in a book titled *Ancient Britain and the Invasions of Julius Caesar* written by T. Rice Holmes and published in 1907. Rice Holmes was an amateur antiquarian and his researches followed on from considerable work on the subject of Caesar's invasions of Britain during the nineteenth century by many others including the investigations by Napoleon Bonaparte's nephew. Ever since Rice Holmes' publication, the academic world has accepted his theories and little further work seems to have been undertaken on the subject.

In essence, following considerable analysis and reasoning, Rice Holmes came to the following conclusions.

Firstly, he stated that the landings in 55 and 54 BC were between Walmer and Deal.[1] He then states that the first battle against the Britons was at Bigbury Camp to the west of Canterbury.[2]

Caesar, he says, then marched all the way to Brentford, crossed the Thames there, then reconnoitred with representatives from the Trinovantes and finally attacked the Catuvellaunian camp at Wheathampstead.

Up to now, this was the full extent of the supposed knowledge of Caesar's movement in Britain. However, Rice Holmes' theories are fraught with inconsistencies and in some cases with clear errors.

Interestingly, Rice Holmes doesn't make mention of any marching camps, but he must have known that an army could not march all the way from the coast to Wheathampstead in one day!

So, let us consider the background to Rice Holmes' conclusions.

Firstly, the landing places. Rice Holmes devotes seventy pages of his book to a consideration of where the landings took place in 55 and 54 BC and he considers in particular many previous theories as to where they may have taken place.[3]

He introduces theories from previous historians which suggest landings anywhere from Pevensey in the west to beyond Dover. Most of Rice Holmes' reasoning hinges on the state of the tides and the direction of the wind, and all this 2,000 years ago. As stated earlier, it is surely impossible to predict where the tides and wind would have been on a single day 2,000 years ago.

Also, the impact of isostatic or post glacial rebound makes the analysis of the shoreline and hinterland impossible to predict after 2,000 years have elapsed.

After seventy pages of detailed analysis, with little basis for reaching any conclusions, Rice Holmes ends this section of his book with the following statement: 'I am sure that the reader is by this time convinced … that it has been demonstrated that he did land both in 55 and 54 BC in East Kent, – in the former year between Walmer Castle and Deal Castle, in the latter north of Deal Castle. That some will still for a time dispute these conclusions is likely enough but not those whose judgements count. For them the problem is solved.'[4]

So there we have it. Job done. No need to question the landing places henceforth. And because of this final statement by Rice Holmes, everyone has accepted his opinion. However, anyone who is prepared to read all those seventy pages of detailed reasoning is entitled to come to the conclusion that the final statement that the problem is solved is merely Rice Holmes' opinion.

Let us now turn to Bigbury as the site where the first battle with the Britons took place.

Interestingly, Rice Holmes puts forward no detailed argument for Bigbury, stating only that it was probably the site of the first battle.[5]

The reasoning for choosing Bigbury, which comes across from various commentators, is that it was obvious as a British camp and well known as such. It was probably the only one known in the area. As mentioned previously, Caesar himself writes that the British retreated to a river before the battle, not over it as Bigbury is. Bigbury is a popular site to ascribe for the first battle but there is no evidence to suggest that it is where the battle was held.

Lastly, let us come to the Thames crossing.

Rice Holmes quotes a Colonel Stoffel who carried out research for Napoleon III as saying that a Thames boatman he consulted told him that between Shepperton and London, there were eight or nine fords across the Thames.[6] Others state that the river was fordable at Chelsea and at Westminster. This does not tally with Caesar's statement that the river was fordable in one place only. Rice Holmes puts a lot of emphasis on the sharp stakes on the riverbank and others in the bed of the river that Caesar mentions and discusses many reports of stakes in the river on many sites in and around the Thames, including Brentford and Hampton.[7] It has to be said that it is unlikely that much if any wood would have survived in the Thames for such a long time.

In fairness to Rice Holmes, he does not state definitively that the crossing was at Brentford but does treat it with a high degree of probability as being the crossing point.

During the march, says Caesar, representatives of the Trinovantes came to see him. As the Trinovantes' territory was north of the Thames, mainly in present day Essex, we must assume that this meeting had taken place after Caesar had crossed the Thames. If he had crossed at Brentford, then either he would have doubled back east a long distance to enter the Trinovante's territory or the Trinovantes would also have travelled a vast distance into hostile Catuvellauni territory to meet Caesar. As the price of acquiring Caesar's protection for the Trinovantes was a large quantity of grain, this would have had to have been transported through hostile territory.

Clearly it does not make sense to travel all the way west to Brentford to cross the river Thames, then march east to meet the Trinovantes then go back to march north west to take the Catuvellaunian camp.

So, to summarise, according to Rice Holmes and therefore the current prevailing view, Caesar landed at Walmer in 55 BC, then again at Deal in 54 BC, marched to Bigbury camp and defeated the Britons, then marched all the way to Brentford where he crossed the Thames then marched east to meet the Trinovantes then marched northwest to take on the Catuvellauni. In all this, Rice Holmes makes no mention of any marching camps.

Chapter Ten

The campaign in Britain – success or failure?

Caesar's campaigns in Britain are often described as a failure. Caesar's only failure. This is no doubt based upon the fact that the invasions did not result in a conquest of the islands as was the case later with the Claudian invasion of 43 AD. But Caesar's was a punitive expedition and as such it was extremely successful, having achieved the objectives he had set himself.

We need to consider why Caesar decided to invade Britain in the first place. In fact, he tells us in his own words. He says that he decided to prepare for an expedition to Britain because he knew that in almost all the Gallic campaigns the Gauls had received reinforcements from the Britons.[1]

There we have it loud and clear. It was not intended to be a conquest, nor a permanent occupation and there was no desire to make Britain part of the Roman Empire as the Roman world would become a few years after Caesar's lifetime. No, it was an expedition to stop the Britons from supporting insurrection in Gaul.

Despite this, a number of theories have been put forward as to why Caesar embarked on the two expeditions to Britain. Some commentators state that having subdued Gaul, Caesar felt he needed another territory to conquer. Others state that Caesar felt under pressure to continue with his process of conquering otherwise he would have been called back to Rome with his job done and with few prospects for him once he had arrived back home. Yet others state that Caesar wanted to conquer Britain so that he would remain in the public eye back home in Rome.

These explanations paint the picture of a Caesar who was concerned constantly about how he would be seen and dealt with by other people. Whilst it is true that earlier in his life, Caesar had had concerns about climbing the greasy pole of Roman politics, his success with the Gallic Wars was such that he was virtually untouchable, and he knew it. This attitude can be seen in his dealing with others, in particular his enemies.

No, we cannot ignore Caesar's own writings and we must accept that the reason why Caesar invaded Britain was that the British had aided some of the tribes Caesar had been fighting against in Gaul and the time had come to punish them and prevent them from ever being a thorn in Caesar's side again. This is what has to be considered in judging whether the two invasions were a success.

What comes through in Caesar's writings is that the main ringleader in Britain was Cassivellaunus who seems to have had power over many other tribes in Britain and may have been the de facto ruler of much of southern Britain. Caesar hints at this by referring at the end of his campaign to the fact that Cassivellaunus was alarmed by so many reverses and by the devastation of his [sic] country. As such, Cassivellaunus would have controlled trade between Britain and the continent and as far as Caesar was concerned would have been a constant thorn in his side.

Let us now consider the first invasion.

Once it became known from information gleaned from cross-Channel traders in Britain that Caesar was planning an invasion, a number of tribes sent envoys who promised to submit to the will of the Romans and to give hostages as security.

Caesar sent Commius whom he had made king of the Atrebates, a tribe in northwest Gaul, back to Britain with those envoys who had come to seek peace with Caesar. Because of the peace agreements, he no doubt felt fairly secure in the thought that many of the British tribes would be submissive once he had invaded.

He probably felt that the only potential hostility would come from Cassivellaunus and therefore he decided to take with him only two legions of approximately 10,000 troops together with some cavalry and others which would have been in total about 12,000 men. This was a reasonably formidable army and certainly one which given Roman military expertise should have been sufficient to defeat one tribe only, the Catuvellauni, of which Cassivellaunus was the leader.

However, the invasion was fraught with difficulties from the start, the worst of which was the duplicity of the Britons who had given the peaceful assurances to Caesar back in Gaul.

We are pretty certain Caesar was planning to land at what is present day Dover as it was by far and away the best harbour and was on the shortest sea route from the continent to Britain.

No doubt, he was very surprised and extremely angry to find that the Britons had lined up for battle on the heights either side of Dover harbour despite their previous peaceful assurances. He had to find somewhere else to land which would not be as dangerous and he travelled seven miles along the coast to find a landing place.

Then the next problem arose. Unable to disembark his troops at a convenient harbour, they had to jump down from the ships which, because of the shallowness of the beach, had meant the ships had had to anchor quite a way out to sea.

The problems didn't stop there. Caesar relied on his cavalry, but they were travelling across the Channel in a violent storm and having been blown off course and despite trying everything possible to make an effective landing, the ships with the cavalry finally had to return to the continent.

This left Caesar with no cavalry, only infantry. However, it doesn't end there, because the violent storm which sent the cavalry off course also wrecked a significant number of the ships the troops had come in.

At this stage, Caesar was facing the very real possibility of being marooned in Britain for the winter.

With this in mind, he decided to live off the land and sent the 7th Legion out to forage for grain. The Britons got to learn of Caesar's predicament and attacked the 7th Legion while they were gathering corn.

The legion and all the troops then retreated to the base camp and waited until the Britons attacked them. When they did, the Romans won the day and beat the Britons off, chasing after them as best they could as all the troops were on foot and would have carried heavy equipment. Nonetheless, a number of the Britons were killed and as an act of revenge, the Romans burnt down every building over a very large area in order to teach the Britons a lesson.

So, was this first invasion successful or a mistake? Surely the only mistake Caesar made was to take the word of the envoys of the Britons who had come to him in Gaul. It is certainly true that the number of misfortunes which occurred presented problems for Caesar which he couldn't have anticipated, and he was unable on this occasion to take on Cassivellaunus.

What the first expedition did achieve, however, was to inform Caesar on what he needed to do on a subsequent occasion, which would be the following year, to achieve the objective he set out with, which was to put down Cassivellaunus and ensure that he would not prove to be a thorn in the side of Rome in the future.

The next invasion in 54 BC was a whole different ball game. Caesar had learnt so much from the expedition the year before and he knew exactly what he needed to do to achieve his objective.

He also took with him, Mandubracius, a prince of the Trinovantes, the arch enemies of the Catuvellauni. Mandubracius almost certainly acted as a guide for Caesar in his march to the Catuvellauni camp.

Caesar took with him five legions, approximately 25,000 men, plus cavalry and support auxiliaries, a total of probably around 30,000 men. This was an absolutely enormous army for the time, but he would need this size of force if he was to travel through hostile territory, and attack Cassivellaunus whilst protecting his rear guard in the process.

It is no wonder that the Britons took fright when they saw the fleet arriving. This was going to be a different invasion from the one the year before.

From here on in, everything went according to plan. There was only one hiccup and that was when the fleet was damaged by a violent storm, again whilst at anchor. This time, Caesar beached his whole fleet of 800 ships and had them repaired whilst he was away campaigning against Cassivellaunus and on this occasion he had the manpower to carry all this out.

Caesar left a legion to guard the base camp, then proceeded to march towards Cassivellaunus' camp. He followed a straight line to the Catuvellauni camp, no doubt using a route already in existence and almost certainly with Mandubracius as guide. He established marching camps at Denge Wood, Kemsley, East Tilbury and Loughton crossing the Thames at East Tilbury.

It is most likely that it was at the camp at East Tilbury, on the border between the Trinovantes and the Catuvellauni, that the envoys from the Trinovantes came to ask Caesar that Mandubracius be made their king and that Caesar release Mandubracius. As usual, the Trinovantes were required to seal their request with a number of hostages and also on this occasion with a quantity of grain. Other tribes when they had heard that the Trinovantes were protected by Caesar sent envoys to surrender and therefore it was now that Caesar could attack the Catuvellauni without hindrance from other tribes. Caesar would have then continued without his guide to establish Loughton Camp which was in the territory of the Catuvellauni.

The tribes who had come to him suing for peace told him that he was not far from Cassivellaunus' stronghold. This meeting probably took place at Loughton Camp or at the nearby Iron Age camp at Ambresbury Banks which was probably a Trinovante encampment, and at that stage Caesar would, most likely, no longer have had Mandubracius as his guide.

He set out for Wheathampstead with either one, or more likely two legions, and sacked the place, driving out the inhabitants. He took booty in the form of cattle and no doubt made the Wheathampstead stronghold into a temporary camp for his legions.

Having sacked Cassivellaunus' headquarters, Caesar retreated back to the coast. However, Cassivellaunus tried once more to rally four tribes from Kent to attack the Roman base camp but they were defeated.

Finally, Cassivellaunus realised that the game was up and surrendered. Interestingly Caesar didn't execute him but let him go, provided he yielded the required number of hostages and paid an annual tribute to Rome.

So, were these two invasions a success? Of course, they were. Caesar's objective was to ensure Cassivellaunus would no longer be a threat to Rome. In this, he succeeded. Caesar never states that he set out to conquer Britain and to bring it into the Roman Empire therefore that can never be a consideration as to whether the invasions had been successful.

It is interesting to note that Caesar refers to the first invasion as an expedition and the second as a campaign. Thus, in no way can the first invasion be looked upon as a failure with the second being undertaken as a result of any errors the year before. The very description of the first invasion as an expedition shows that Caesar regarded it as an exploratory invasion made in order to establish just exactly what would be needed for a full-blown invasion and campaign.

The second invasion succeeded in achieving its objectives. The much-increased size of the invasion fleet was enough to frighten off the Britons and therefore enable Caesar to land at the best possible place in Britain. The overland march was a classic exercise in campaigning, with marching camps constructed a day's march from each other and manned permanently by a strong force of troops, a route in a straight line so as not to waste marching time and a swift and a successful attack on the headquarters of the leader of the enemy forces.

Caesar had no wish nor need to occupy Britain. He merely set out to conquer those who were giving aid to his enemies in Gaul and ensure that they would cease to be a thorn in his side.

Cassivellaunus eventually surrendered to Caesar, provided the hostages which Caesar had demanded and undertook to pay an annual tribute to Rome; although this payment was not chased up and eventually lapsed, probably as a result of Caesar's death only ten years later.

Chapter Eleven

Britain after Caesar

Britain would never be the same again after Caesar left in 54 BC. Cassivellaunus, the dominant leader of the strongest tribe, the Catuvellauni, had been defeated by the Romans. Other tribes had been subdued and tributes demanded of them. Although not conquered as such, Britain was a defeated Island.

Attempts would have been made to return to normal after the Romans had left, but the world around them was changing for the Britons. Within a matter of a few years, the whole of Gaul would be conquered by the Romans and become a Roman province within the empire, and it was with that empire that the British had to conduct almost all their external relations.

Caesar left Britain in 54 BC after his defeat of the Catuvellauni with hostages and instructions that the Britons should pay an annual tribute to Rome and that the Catuvellauni should also not attack the Trinovantes.

Caesar was very busy and preoccupied in the ten years between his second invasion of Britain and his assassination in 44 BC and no doubt felt that issues regarding Britain were no longer significant.

As far as is known, the tribute was never paid and, furthermore, the Catuvellauni not only took over the Trinovante lands but they also drove the tribe out of their territory. In the period between the two invasions, the Catuvellauni acquired territory in much of East Anglia and south-east England to the extent that the historian Suetonius, writing in the late first century, described Cunobelinus, who was the leader of the Catuvellauni by the 40s BC as the King of Britain.[1]

In the ninety-seven years between Caesar's invasion and the Claudian invasion of 43 AD, there was considerable change in Britain.

With Gaul by then a full Roman province all trade between Britain and the continent was effectively trade with Rome. Archaeological evidence has revealed that this trade was continuously increasing. The grain being grown in Britain was far in excess of the needs of the population, which indicates that there was a healthy and sophisticated export market.

Britain was now living in a world which was dominated by the power of Rome and it increasingly adopted Roman fashions and practices. For example, coins began to be minted in the style of Roman coins. Some of these were minted by the successors of Commius, who had become chief of the British Atrebates after having fled from Caesar in northern Gaul. By 43 AD, British tribes had adopted Roman titles and looked to the Emperor in Rome to settle disputes. The fact is that the British had become highly Romanised even before the Claudian invasion.

Rome considered the possibility of another invasion from time to time and Dio Cassius writing in the late second century AD states that plans were made on three occasions, 34, 27 and 26 BC. Nothing came of these plans which may have been to enforce the payment of the tribute promised to Caesar. However, it is also possible that the Emperor Augustus took the view that the costs of occupying Britain would outweigh the benefits of customs duties which Rome was already earning on trade with Britain. In other words, it would be more profitable to maintain the status quo.

In 39 AD, the then leader of the Catuvellauni, Cunobelinus, expelled his son, Adminius, who then fled to Rome to seek the protection of the Emperor Gaius, now known generally as Caligula. Caligula saw this tension in Britain as a perfect opportunity to invade. Detailed planning and construction work was undertaken and only at the last minute was the invasion called off.

In the meantime, sometime between 39 AD and 43 AD, Cunobelinus died and there was evidence that Britain was becoming hostile towards Rome. Caligula himself had died in 41 AD and his successor Claudius decided to invade Britain, and probably took the opportunity to use all the planning and construction work already done by Caligula.[2]

Claudius invaded with four legions, together with the same number of auxiliary troops. Even though initially, the troops had shown themselves to have been in fear of invading Britain, the invasion went ahead, was a success and Colchester, by then the capital of the Catuvellauni, was taken by the Romans.

The fact that he managed to conquer Britain with only four legions compared with the five that Caesar brought over in 54 BC is a clear indication of the extent to which Britain had become a vassal state of Rome in the intervening period between the two invasions. Caesar had encountered hostile tribes, whereas Claudius' army invaded what was a major trading partner of Rome.

The Romans spread out throughout the country and considerable success and progress was made. Within ten years of the invasion, much of the south was in Roman hands and the main road from the south west to the north, the Fosse Way, had been constructed.

Britain was now a Roman province and would remain so for nearly 400 years.

It is tempting to look at Roman Britain as a country with a settled life of large villas, opulent towns and a thriving farming industry. Some of this is true but, by and large, the period between the Claudian invasion and the end of Roman rule in the fifth century saw a succession of rebellions, invasions and general hardship.

One of the earliest actions of the Romans after the invasion was to disarm all the British tribes. The Romans had a rule that civilians were not allowed to bear arms. This did not go down well and in due course, the Iceni of Norfolk rebelled, following appalling behaviour by local Roman officials who had had their leader Boudicca flogged and her daughters raped.

The rebellion was put down by the Romans but not before London and Verulamium (modern day St Albans) had been razed and their inhabitants slaughtered. As a result of the rebellion, the Emperor Nero even considered abandoning Britain altogether.

British tribes continued to harry the Romans throughout the years of the occupation, particularly in the form of rebellions by the Brigantes in the north. The Emperor Hadrian had a wall built to create a border between Roman-occupied Britain and the unoccupied north of the country. In time the wall would function mainly just as a customs post. For a while there was an earthen wall constructed between the Forth and the Clyde under the Emperor

Antonine but although attempts were made to colonise Scotland these were never successful and the wall, known as the Antonine Wall was eventually abandoned and the Romans withdrew to Hadrian's Wall.

Although we talk of Roman Britain, the bulk of the population was British, and the term Romano-British is best used to describe the population. London became the business centre of Roman Britain and most Roman roads spread out from London. It later became the capital.

Ultimate governance of the province would have been exercised from Rome but, over the years of occupation, there were a multitude of emperors, some with limited areas of influence and on a number of occasions renegades set themselves up as emperors of Britain alone, in defiance of Rome.

As the centuries passed, there were an increasing number of raids by what the Romans called pirates. The Romans called all ship-based enemies pirates. These would have been Saxons, Angles, Franks, Picts, Scots and the Attacotti who were probably from lowland Scotland.

Life for the average Romano-Briton was unsettled and if we add to that the fact that the currency suffered rampant inflation in the third century and that the population suffered plagues from time to time, life must have been very hard.

For some, life did improve under the Roman occupation. Towards the end of Roman rule, there is evidence that villas, particularly in east Anglia, were displaying considerable wealth.[3]

It must, therefore, have come as a massive shock when the Roman empire started disintegrating in the early fifth century mainly as a result of the barbarian attacks on all quarters of the Empire, although sporadic attacks had begun as early as the third century and in the fourth century the Picts and the Scots had raided the northern frontier.

In 410, the Emperor Honorius wrote to the British telling them that Rome could no longer provide a defence force for Britain and therefore Britain was effectively on its own. Attacks continued, particularly from the Saxons, although some of these were successfully repelled. Myres in his book *The English Settlements* states that by the end of the fifth century, Romanized life in the cities had been completely destroyed.[4] If this was indeed the case, then only two scenarios can be assumed for the population of those cities. Either they had left to live in the countryside, but it is questionable how they would manage to leave a civilised environment with proper brick-constructed buildings and go back to living in round houses, or what is more likely is that they were massacred by the invaders.

In the ensuing centuries, the country was invaded and settled by Saxons and Vikings. Other invasions occurred, among which were the Normans in 1066, the French in 1216 and the Dutch in 1688.

Today there are still many reminders of Roman Britain to be seen, from the ruins of Hadrian's Wall to the well preserved Roman Baths at Bath. The earliest buildings still in occupation date from Saxon times and there are no longer any Roman buildings occupied in Britain.

One interesting reminder of Roman Britain can still be found over much of the countryside and is often overlooked for want of understanding as to what it means. Around the country there are many places called Coldharbour.[5] This name has Saxon roots and means an abandoned structure near a road where a traveller could shelter for the night. In Saxon times, these abandoned structures could only have been derelict Roman buildings, perhaps the remains of Mansios, which were Roman way-side inns or maybe derelict villas which had nearly always been built close to Roman roads.

This means that whenever we see the name Coldharbour on a map or on a sign, we can know that we are almost certainly very close to the site of a Roman building and knowing this can take us back in our minds in a direct line to the occupation of Britain by the Romans, the beginning of which was started over 2,000 years ago by one of the greatest generals in history, Julius Caesar.

Appendix One

The Gallic Wars

By Julius Caesar
*Adapted from the translation by W.A. McDevitte
and W.S. Bohn*

Book 4

Chapter 20

During the short part of summer which remained, Caesar, although in these countries, as all Gaul lies toward the north, the winters are early, nevertheless resolved to proceed into Britain, because he discovered that in almost all the wars with the Gauls succours had been furnished to our enemy from that country; and even if the time of year should be insufficient for carrying on the war, yet he thought it would be of great service to him if he only entered the island, and saw into the character of the people, and got knowledge of their localities, harbours, and landing-places, all which were for the most part unknown to the Gauls. For neither does anyone except merchants generally go thither, nor even to them was any portion of it known, except the sea-coast and those parts which are opposite to Gaul. Therefore, after having called up to him the merchants from all parts, he could learn neither what was the size of the island, nor what or how numerous were the nations which inhabited it, nor what system of war they followed, nor what customs they used, nor what harbours were convenient for a great number of large ships.

Chapter 21

He sends before him Caius Volusenus with a ship of war, to acquire a knowledge of these particulars before he, in person, should make a descent into the island, as he was convinced that this was a judicious measure. He commissioned him to thoroughly examine into all matters, and then return to him as soon as possible. He himself proceeds to the Morini with all his forces. He orders ships from all parts of the neighbouring countries, and the fleet which the preceding summer he had built for the war with the Veneti, to assemble in this place. In the meantime, his purpose having been discovered, and reported to the Britons by merchants, ambassadors come to him from several states of the island, to promise that they will give hostages, and submit to the government of the Roman people. Having given them an audience, he, after promising liberally, and exhorting them to continue in that purpose, sends them back to their own country, and [dispatches] with them Commius, whom, upon subduing the Atrebates, he had created king there, a man whose courage and conduct he esteemed, and who he thought would be faithful to him, and whose influence ranked highly in those countries. He orders him to visit as many states as he could and persuade them to embrace the protection of the Roman people, and apprize them that he would shortly come thither. Volusenus, having viewed the localities as far as means could be afforded one who dared not leave his ship and trust himself to barbarians, returns to Caesar on the fifth day, and reports what he had there observed.

Chapter 22

While Caesar remains in these parts for the purpose of procuring ships, ambassadors come to him from a great portion of the Morini, to plead their excuse respecting their conduct on the late occasion; alleging that it was as men uncivilized, and as those who were unacquainted with our custom, that they had made war upon the Roman people, and promising to perform what he should command. Caesar, thinking that this had happened fortunately enough for him, because he neither wished to leave an enemy behind him, nor had an opportunity for carrying on a war, by reason of the time of year, nor considered that employment in such trifling matters was to be preferred to his enterprise on Britain, imposes a large number of hostages; and when these were brought, he received them to his protection. Having collected together, and provided about eighty transport ships, as many as he thought necessary for conveying over two legions, he assigned such [ships] of war as he had besides to the quaestor [officials who had charge of public revenue and expenditure], his lieutenants, and officers of cavalry. There were in addition to these eighteen ships of burden which were prevented, eight miles from that place, by winds, from being able to reach the same port. These he distributed among the horse; the rest of the army, he delivered to Q. Titurius Sabinus and L. Aurunculeius Cotta, his lieutenants, to lead into the territories of the Menapii and those cantons of the Morini from which ambassadors had not come to him. He ordered P. Sulpicius Rufus, his lieutenant, to hold possession of the harbour, with such a garrison as he thought sufficient.

Chapter 23

These matters being arranged, finding the weather favourable for his voyage, he set sail about the third watch, and ordered the horse to march forward to the further port, and there embark and follow him. As this was performed rather tardily by them, he himself reached Britain with the first squadron of ships, about the fourth hour of the day, and there saw the forces of the enemy drawn up in arms on all the hills. The nature of the place was this: the sea was confined by mountains so close to it that a dart could be thrown from their summit upon the shore. Considering this by no means a fit place for disembarking, he remained at anchor till the ninth hour, for the other ships to arrive there. Having in the meantime assembled the lieutenants and military tribunes, he told them both what he had learned from Volusenus, and what he wished to be done; and enjoined them (as the principle of military matters, and especially as maritime affairs, which have a precipitate and uncertain action, required) that all things should be performed by them at a nod and at the instant. Having dismissed them, meeting both with wind and tide favourable at the same time, the signal being given and the anchor weighed, he advanced about seven miles from that place, and stationed his fleet over against an open and level shore.

Chapter 24

But the barbarians, upon perceiving the design of the Romans, sent forward their cavalry and charioteers, a class of warriors of whom it is their practice to make great use in their battles, and following with the rest of their forces, endeavoured to prevent our men landing. In this was the greatest difficulty, for the following reasons, namely, because our ships, on account of their great size, could be stationed only in deep water; and our soldiers, in places unknown to them, with their hands embarrassed, oppressed with a large and heavy weight of armour, had at the same time to leap from the ships, stand amid the waves, and encounter the enemy; whereas they, either on dry ground, or advancing a little way into the water, free in all their limbs in places thoroughly known to them, could confidently throw their weapons and spur on their horses, which were accustomed to this kind of service. Dismayed by these circumstances and altogether untrained in this mode of battle, our men did not all exert the same vigour and eagerness which they had been wont to exert in engagements on dry ground.

Chapter 25

When Caesar observed this, he ordered the ships of war, the appearance of which was somewhat strange to the barbarians and the motion more ready for service, to be withdrawn a little from the transport vessels, and to be propelled by their oars, and be stationed toward the open flank of the enemy, and the enemy to be beaten off and driven away, with slings, arrows, and engines: which plan was of great service to our men; for the barbarians being startled by the form of our ships and the motions of our oars and the nature of our engines, which was strange to them, stopped, and shortly after retreated a little. And while our men were hesitating [whether they should advance to the shore], chiefly on account of the depth of the sea, he who carried the eagle of the tenth legion, after supplicating the gods that the matter might turn out favourably to the legion, exclaimed, 'Leap, fellow soldiers, unless you wish to betray your eagle to the enemy. I, for my part, will perform my duty to the commonwealth and my general.' When he had said this with a loud voice, he leaped from the ship and proceeded to bear the eagle toward the enemy. Then our men, exhorting one another that so great a disgrace should not be incurred, all leaped from the ship. When those in the nearest vessels saw them, they speedily followed and approached the enemy.

Chapter 26

The battle was maintained vigorously on both sides. Our men, however, as they could neither keep their ranks, nor get firm footing, nor follow their standards, and as one from one ship and another from another assembled around whatever standards they met, were thrown into great confusion. But the enemy, who were acquainted with all the shallows, when from the shore they saw any coming from a ship one by one, spurred on their horses, and attacked them while embarrassed; many surrounded a few, others threw their weapons upon our collected forces on their exposed flank. When Caesar observed this, he ordered the boats of the ships of war and the spy sloops to be filled with soldiers, and sent them up to the succour of those whom he had observed in distress. Our men, as soon as they made good their footing on dry ground, and all their comrades had joined them, made an attack upon the enemy, and put them to flight, but could not pursue them very far, because the horses had not been able to maintain their course at sea and reach the island. This alone was wanting to Caesar's accustomed success.

Chapter 27

The enemy being thus vanquished in battle, as soon as they recovered after their flight, instantly sent ambassadors to Caesar to negotiate peace. They promised to give hostages and perform what he should command. Together with these ambassadors came Commius the Altrebatian, who, as I have above said, had been sent by Caesar into Britain. Him they had seized upon when leaving his ship, although in the character of ambassador he bore the general's commission to them, and thrown into chains: then after the battle was fought, they sent him back, and in suing for peace cast the blame of that act upon the common people, and entreated that it might be pardoned on account of their indiscretion. Caesar, complaining, that after they had sued for peace, and had voluntarily sent ambassadors into the continent for that purpose, they had made war without a reason, said that he would pardon their indiscretion, and imposed hostages, a part of whom they gave immediately; the rest they said they would give in a few days, since they were sent for from remote places. In the meantime they ordered their people to return to the country parts, and the chiefs assembled from all quarters, and proceeded to surrender themselves and their states to Caesar.

Chapter 28

A peace being established by these proceedings four days after we had come into Britain, the eighteen ships, to which reference has been made above, and which conveyed the cavalry, set sail from the upper port with a gentle gale, when, however, they were approaching Britain and were seen from the camp, so great a storm suddenly arose that none of them could maintain their course at sea; and some were taken back to the same port from which they had started; others, to their great danger, were driven to the lower part of the island, nearer to the west; which, however, after having cast anchor, as they were getting filled with water, put out to sea through necessity in a stormy night, and made for the continent.

Chapter 29

It happened that night to be full moon, which usually occasions very high tides in that ocean; and that circumstance was unknown to our men. Thus, at the same time, the tide began to fill the ships of war which Caesar had provided to convey over his army, and which he had drawn up on the strand; and the storm began to dash the ships of burden which were riding at anchor against each other; nor was any means afforded our men of either managing them or of rendering any service. A great many ships having been wrecked, inasmuch as the rest, having lost their cables, anchors, and other tackling, were unfit for sailing, a great confusion, as would necessarily happen, arose throughout the army; for there were no other ships in which they could be conveyed back, and all things which are of service in repairing vessels were wanting, and, corn for the winter had not been provided in those places, because it was understood by all that they would certainly winter in Gaul.

Chapter 30

On discovering these things the chiefs of Britain, who had come up after the battle was fought to perform those conditions which Caesar had imposed, held a conference, when they perceived that cavalry, and ships, and corn were wanting to the Romans, and discovered the small number of our soldiers from the small extent of the camp (which, too, was on this account more limited than ordinary, because Caesar had conveyed over his legions without baggage), and thought that the best plan was to renew the war, and cut off our men from corn and provisions and protract the affair till winter; because they felt confident, that, if they were vanquished or cut off from a return, no one would afterward pass over into Britain for the purpose of making war. Therefore, again entering into a conspiracy, they began to depart from the camp by degrees and secretly bring up their people from the country parts.

Chapter 31

But Caesar, although he had not as yet discovered their measures, yet, both from what had occurred to his ships, and from the circumstance that they had neglected to give the promised hostages, suspected that the thing would come to pass which really did happen. He therefore provided remedies against all contingencies; for he daily conveyed corn from the country parts into the camp, used the timber and brass of such ships as were most seriously damaged for repairing the rest, and ordered whatever things besides were necessary for this object to be brought to him from the continent. And thus, since that business was executed by the soldiers with the greatest energy, he effected that, after the loss of twelve ships, a voyage could be made well enough in the rest.

Chapter 32

While these things are being transacted, one legion had been sent to forage, according to custom, and no suspicion of war had arisen as yet, and some of the people remained in the country parts, others went backward and forward to the camp, they who were on duty at the gates of the camp reported to Caesar that a greater dust than was usual was seen in that direction in which the legion had marched. Caesar, suspecting that which was [really the case] – that some new enterprise was undertaken by the barbarians, ordered the two cohorts which were on duty, to march into that quarter with him, and two other cohorts to relieve them on duty; the rest to be armed and follow him immediately. When he had advanced some little way from the camp, he saw that his men were overpowered by the enemy and scarcely able to stand their ground, and that, the legion being crowded together, weapons were being cast on them from all sides. For as all the corn was reaped in every part with the exception of one, the enemy, suspecting that our men would repair to that, had concealed themselves in the woods during the night. Then attacking them suddenly, scattered as they were, and when they had laid aside their arms, and were engaged in reaping, they killed a small number, threw the rest into confusion, and surrounded them with their cavalry and chariots.

Chapter 33

Their mode of fighting with their chariots is this: firstly, they drive about in all directions and throw their weapons and generally break the ranks of the enemy with the very dread of their horses and the noise of their wheels; and when they have worked themselves in between the troops of horse, leap from their chariots and engage on foot. The charioteers in the meantime withdraw some little distance from the battle, and so place themselves with the chariots that, if their masters are overpowered by the number of the enemy, they may have a ready retreat to their own troops. Thus they display in battle the speed of horse, [together with] the firmness of infantry; and by daily practice and exercise attain to such expertness that they are accustomed, even on a declining and steep place, to check their horses at full speed, and manage and turn them in an instant and run along the pole, and stand on the yoke, and thence betake themselves with the greatest celerity to their chariots again.

Chapter 34

Under these circumstances, our men being dismayed by the novelty of this mode of battle, Caesar most seasonably brought assistance; for upon his arrival the enemy paused, and our men recovered from their fear; upon which thinking the time unfavourable for provoking the enemy and coming to an action, he kept himself in his own quarter, and, a short time having intervened, drew back the legions into the camp. While these things are going on, and all our men engaged, the rest of the Britons, who were in the fields, departed. Storms then set in for several successive days, which both confined our men to the camp and hindered the enemy from attacking us. In the meantime the barbarians dispatched messengers to all parts, and reported to their people the small number of our soldiers, and how good an opportunity was given for obtaining spoil and for liberating themselves forever, if they should only drive the Romans from their camp. Having by these means speedily got together a large force of infantry and of cavalry they came up to the camp.

Chapter 35

Although Caesar anticipated that the same thing which had happened on former occasions would then occur – that, if the enemy were routed, they would escape from danger by their speed; still, having got about thirty horse, which Commius the Atrebatian, of whom mention has been made, had brought over with him [from Gaul], he drew up the legions in order of battle before the camp. When the action commenced, the enemy were unable to sustain the attack of our men for long and turned their backs; our men pursued them as far as their speed and strength permitted, and slew a great number of them; then, having destroyed and burned everything far and wide, they retreated to their camp.

Chapter 36

The same day, ambassadors sent by the enemy came to Caesar to negotiate a peace. Caesar doubled the number of hostages which he had before demanded; and ordered that they should be brought over to the continent, because, since the time of the equinox was near, he did not consider that, with his ships out of repair, the voyage ought to be deferred till winter. Having met with favourable weather, he set sail a little after midnight, and all his fleet arrived safe at the continent, except two of the ships of burden which could not make the same port which the other ships did, and were carried a little lower down.

Chapter 37

When our soldiers, about 300 in number, had been drawn out of these two ships, and were marching to the camp, the Morini, whom Caesar, when setting forth for Britain, had left in a state of peace, excited by the hope of spoil, at first surrounded them with a small number of men, and ordered them to lay down their arms, if they did not wish to be slain; afterward however, when they, forming a circle, stood on their defence, a shout was raised and about 6,000 of the enemy soon assembled; which being reported, Caesar sent all the cavalry in the camp as a relief to his men. In the meantime our soldiers sustained the attack of the enemy, and fought most valiantly for more than four hours, and, receiving but few wounds themselves, slew several of them. But after our cavalry came in sight, the enemy, throwing away their arms, turned their backs, and a great number of them were killed.

Chapter 38

The day following Caesar sent Labienus, his lieutenant, with those legions which he had brought back from Britain, against the Morini, who had revolted; who, as they had no place to which they might retreat, on account of the drying up of their marshes (which they had availed themselves of as a place of refuge the preceding year), almost all fell into the power of Labienus. In the meantime Caesar's lieutenants, Q. Titurius and L. Cotta, who had led the legions into the territories of the Menapii, having laid waste all their lands, cut down their corn and burned their houses, returned to Caesar because the Menapii had all concealed themselves in their thickest woods. Caesar fixed the winter quarters of all the legions among the Belgae. Thither only two British states sent hostages; the rest omitted to do so. For these successes, a thanksgiving of twenty days was decreed by the senate upon receiving Caesar's letter.

The Gallic Wars

By Julius Caesar
Adapted from the translation by W. A. McDevitte and W. S. Bohn

Book 5

Chapter 1

Lucius Domitius and Appius Claudius being consuls, Caesar, when departing from his winter quarters into Italy, as he had been accustomed to do yearly, commands the lieutenants whom he appointed over the legions to take care that during the winter as many ships as possible should be built, and the old repaired. He plans the size and shape of them. For dispatch of lading, and for drawing them on shore, he makes them a little lower than those which we have been accustomed to use in our sea; and that so much the more, because he knew that, on account of the frequent changes of the tide, less swells occurred there; for the purpose of transporting burdens and a great number of horses, [he makes them] a little broader than those which we use in other seas. All these he orders to be constructed for lightness and expedition, to which object their lowness contributes greatly. He orders those things which are necessary for equipping ships to be brought thither from Spain. He himself, on the assizes of Hither Gaul being concluded, proceeds into Illyricum, because he heard that the part of the province nearest them was being laid waste by the incursions of the Pirustae. When he had arrived there, he levies soldiers upon the states, and orders them to assemble at an appointed place. Which circumstance having been reported [to them], the Pirustae send ambassadors to him to inform him that no part of those proceedings was done by public deliberation and assert that they were ready to make compensation by all means for the injuries [inflicted]. Caesar, accepting their defence, demands hostages, and orders them to be brought to him on a specified day, and assures them that unless they did so he would visit their state with war. These being brought to him on the day which he had ordered, he appoints arbitrators between the states, who should estimate the damages and determine the reparation.

Chapter 2

These things being finished, and the assizes being concluded, he returns into Hither Gaul, and proceeds thence to the army. When he had arrived there, having made a survey of the winter quarter, he finds that, by the extraordinary labour of the soldiers, amid the utmost scarcity of all materials, about six hundred ships of that kind which we have described above and twenty-eight ships of war, had been built, and were not far from that state, that they might be launched in a few days. Having commended the soldiers and those who had presided over the work, he informs them what he wishes to be done, and orders all the ships to assemble at port Itius, from which port he had learned that the passage into Britain was shortest, [being only] about thirty miles from the continent. He left what seemed a sufficient number of soldiers for that design; he himself proceeds into the territories of the Treviri with four legions without baggage, and 800 horse, because they neither came to the general diets [of Gaul], nor obeyed his commands, and were moreover, said to be tampering with the Germans beyond the Rhine.

Chapter 3

This state is by far the most powerful of all Gaul in cavalry, and has great forces of infantry, and as we have remarked above, borders on the Rhine. In that state, two persons, Indutiomarus and Cingetorix, were then contending with each other for the supreme power; one of whom, as soon as the arrival of Caesar and his legions was known, came to him; assures him that he and all his party would continue in their allegiance, and not revolt from the alliance of the Roman people, and informs him of the things which were going on among the Treviri. But Indutiomarus began to collect cavalry and infantry, and make preparations for war, having concealed those who by reason of their age could not be under arms, in the forest Arduenna, which is of immense size, [and] extends from the Rhine across the country of the Treviri to the frontiers of the Remi. But after that, some of the chief persons of the state, both influenced by their friendship for Cingetorix, and alarmed at the arrival of our army, came to Caesar and began to solicit him privately about their own interests, since they could not provide for the safety of the state; Indutiomarus, dreading lest he should be abandoned by all, sends ambassadors to Caesar, to declare that he absented himself from his countrymen, and refrained from coming to him on this account, that he might the more easily keep the state in its allegiance, lest on the departure of all the nobility the commonalty should, in their indiscretion, revolt. And thus, the whole state was at his control; and that he, if Caesar would permit, would come to the camp to him, and would commit his own fortunes and those of the state to his good faith.

Chapter 4

Caesar, though he discerned from what motive these things were said, and what circumstances deterred him from his meditated plan, still, in order that he might not be compelled to waste the summer among the Treviri, while all things were prepared for the war with Britain, ordered Indutiomarus to come to him with 200 hostages. When they were brought, [and] among them his son and near relations, whom he had demanded by name, he consoled Indutiomarus, and enjoined him to continue in his allegiance; yet, nevertheless, summoning to him the chief men of the Treviri, he reconciled them individually to Cingetorix: this he both thought should be done by him in justice to the merits of the latter, and also judged that it was of great importance that the influence of one whose singular attachment toward him he had fully seen, should prevail as much as possible among his people. Indutiomarus was very much offended at this act, [seeing that] his influence was diminished among his countrymen; and he, who already before had borne a hostile mind toward us, was much more violently inflamed against us through resentment at this.

Chapter 5

These matters being settled, Caesar went to port Itius with the legions. There he discovers that forty ships, which had been built in the country of the Meldi, having been driven back by a storm, had been unable to maintain their course, and had returned to the same port from which they had set out; he finds the rest ready for sailing, and furnished with everything. In the same place, the cavalry of the whole of Gaul, in number 4,000, assembles, and [also] the chief persons of all the states; he had determined to leave in Gaul a very few of them, whose fidelity toward him he had clearly discerned, and take the rest with him as hostages; because he feared a commotion in Gaul when he should be absent.

Chapter 6

There was together with the others, Dumnorix, the Aeduan, of whom we have made previous mention. Him, in particular, he had resolved to have with him, because he had discovered him to be fond of change, fond of power, possessing great resolution, and great influence among the Gauls. To this was added, that Dumnorix had before said in an assembly of Aeduans, that the sovereignty of the state had been made over to him by Caesar; which speech the Aedui bore with impatience and yet dared not send ambassadors to Caesar for the purpose of either rejecting or deprecating [that appointment]. That fact Caesar had learned from his own personal friends. He at first strove to obtain by every entreaty that he should be left in Gaul; partly, because, being unaccustomed to sailing, he feared the sea; partly because he said he was prevented by divine admonitions. After he saw that this request was firmly refused him, all hope of success being lost, he began to tamper with the chief persons of the Gauls, to call them apart singly and exhort them to remain on the continent; to agitate them with the fear that it was not without reason that Gaul should be stripped of all her nobility; that it was Caesar's design, to bring over to Britain and put to death all those whom he feared to slay in the sight of Gaul, to pledge his honour to the rest, to ask for their oath that they would by common deliberation execute what they should perceive to be necessary for Gaul. These things were reported to Caesar by several persons.

122

Chapter 7

Having learned this fact, Caesar, because he had conferred so much honour upon the Aeduan state, determined that Dumnorix should be restrained and deterred by whatever means he could; and that, because he perceived his insane designs to be proceeding further and further, care should be taken lest he might be able to injure him and the commonwealth. Therefore, having stayed about twenty-five days in that place, because the north wind, which usually blows a great part of every season, prevented the voyage, he exerted himself to keep Dumnorix in his allegiance [and] nevertheless learn all his measures: having at length met with favourable weather, he orders the foot soldiers and the horse to embark in the ships. But, while the minds of all were occupied, Dumnorix began to take his departure from the camp homeward with the cavalry of the Aedui, Caesar being ignorant of it. Caesar, on this matter being reported to him, ceasing from his expedition and deferring all other affairs, sends a great part of the cavalry to pursue him, and commands that he be brought back; he orders that if he uses violence and does not submit, that he be slain; considering that Dumnorix would do nothing as a rational man while he himself was absent, since he had disregarded his command even when present. He, however, when recalled, began to resist and defend himself with his hand, and implore the support of his people, often exclaiming that 'he was free and the subject of a free state'. They surround and kill the man as they had been commanded; but the Aeduan horsemen all returned to Caesar.

Chapter 8

When these things were done [and] Labienus, left on the continent with three legions and 2,000 horse, to defend the harbours and provide corn, and discover what was going on in Gaul, and take measures according to the occasion and according to the circumstance; he himself, with five legions and a number of horse, equal to that which he was leaving on the continent, set sail at sun-set, and [though for a time] borne forward by a gentle south-west wind, he did not maintain his course, in consequence of the wind dying away about midnight, and being carried on too far by the tide, when the sun rose, espied Britain passed on his left. Then, again, following the change of tide, he urged on with the oars that he might make that part of the island in which he had discovered the preceding summer, that there was the best landing-places, and in this affair the spirit of our soldiers was very much to be extolled; for they with the transports and heavy ships, the labour of rowing not being [for a moment] discontinued, equalled the speed of the ships of war. All the ships reached Britain nearly at mid-day; nor was there seen a [single] enemy in that place, but, as Caesar afterward found from some prisoners, though large bodies of troops had assembled there, yet being alarmed by the great number of our ships, more than eight hundred of which, including the ships of the preceding year, and those private vessels which each had built for his own convenience, had appeared at one time, they had quitted the coast and concealed themselves among the higher points.

Chapter 9

Caesar, having disembarked his army and chosen a convenient place for the camp, when he discovered from the prisoners in what part the forces of the enemy had lodged themselves, having left ten cohorts and 300 horse at the sea, to be a guard to the ships, hastens to the enemy, at the third watch, fearing the less for the ships, for this reason because he was leaving them fastened at anchor upon an even and open shore; and he placed Q. Atrius over the guard of the ships. He himself, having advanced by night about twelve miles, espied the forces of the enemy. They, advancing to the river with their cavalry and chariots from the higher ground, began to annoy our men and give battle. Being repulsed by our cavalry, they concealed themselves in woods, as they had secured a place admirably fortified by nature and by art, which, as it seemed, they had before prepared on account of a civil war; for all entrances to it were shut up by a great number of felled trees. They themselves rushed out of the woods to fight here and there, and prevented our men from entering their fortifications. But the soldiers of the seventh legion, having formed a testudo and thrown up a rampart against the fortification, took the place and drove them out of the woods, receiving only a few wounds. But Caesar forbade his men to pursue them in their flight any great distance; both because he was ignorant of the nature of the ground, and because, as a great part of the day was spent, he wished time to be left for the fortification of the camp.

Chapter 10

The next day, early in the morning, he sent both foot-soldiers and horse in three divisions on an expedition to pursue those who had fled. These having advanced a little way, when already the rear [of the enemy] was in sight, some horse came to Caesar from Quintus Atrius, to report that the preceding night, a very great storm having arisen, almost all the ships were dashed to pieces and cast upon the shore, because neither the anchors and cables could resist, nor could the sailors and pilots sustain the violence of the storm; and thus great damage was received by that collision of the ships.

Chapter 11

These things being known [to him], Caesar orders the legions and cavalry to be recalled and to cease from their march; he himself returns to the ships: he sees clearly before him almost the same things which he had heard of from the messengers and by letter, so that, about forty ships being lost, the remainder seemed capable of being repaired with much labour. Therefore, he selects workmen from the legions, and orders others to be sent for from the continent; he writes to Labienus to build as many ships as he could with those legions which were with him. He himself, though the matter was one of great difficulty and labour, yet thought it to be most expedient for all the ships to be brought up on shore and joined with the camp by one fortification. In these matters he employed about ten days, the labour of the soldiers being unremitting even during the hours of night. The ships having been brought up on shore and the camp strongly fortified, he left the same forces as he did before as a guard for the ships; he sets out in person for the same place that he had returned from. When he had come thither, greater forces of the Britons had already assembled at that place, the chief command and management of the war having been intrusted to Cassivellaunus, whose territories a river, which is called the Thames, separates, from the maritime states at about eighty miles from the sea. At an earlier period, perpetual wars had taken place between him and the other states; but, greatly alarmed by our arrival, the Britons had placed him over the whole war and the conduct of it.

Chapter 12

The interior portion of Britain is inhabited by those of whom they say that it is handed down by tradition that they were born in the island itself: the maritime portion by those who had passed over from the country of the Belgae for the purpose of plunder and making war; almost all of whom are called by the names of those states from which they sprung, and having waged war, continued there and began to cultivate the lands. The number of the people is countless, and their buildings exceedingly numerous, for the most part very like those of the Gauls: the number of cattle is great. They use either brass or iron rings, determined at a certain weight, as their money. Tin is produced in the midland regions; in the maritime, iron; but the quantity of it is small: they employ brass, which is imported. There, as in Gaul, is timber of every description, except beech and fir. They do not regard it lawful to eat the hare, and the cock, and the goose; they, however, breed them for amusement and pleasure. The climate is more temperate than in Gaul, the colds being less severe.

Chapter 13

The island is triangular in its form, and one of its sides is opposite to Gaul. One angle of this side, which is in Kent, whither almost all ships from Gaul are directed, [looks] to the east; the lower looks to the south. This side extends about 500 miles. Another side lies toward Spain and the west, on which part is Ireland, less, as is reckoned, than Britain, by one half: but the passage [from it] into Britain is of equal distance with that from Gaul. In the middle of this voyage, is an island, which is called Mona: many smaller islands besides are supposed to lie [there], of which islands some have written that at the time of the winter solstice it is night there for thirty consecutive days. We, in our inquiries about that matter, ascertained nothing, except that, by accurate measurements with water, we perceived the nights to be shorter there than on the continent. The length of this side, as their account states, is

700 miles. The third side is toward the north, to which portion of the island no land is opposite; but an angle of that side looks principally toward Germany. This side is considered to be 800 miles in length. Thus, the whole island is [about] 2,000 miles in circumference.

Chapter 14

The most civilized of all these nations are they who inhabit Kent, which is entirely a maritime district, nor do they differ much from the Gallic customs. Most of the inland inhabitants do not sow corn, but live on milk and flesh, and are clad with skins. All the Britains, indeed, dye themselves with woad, which occasions a bluish colour, and thereby have a more terrible appearance in fight. They wear their hair long and have every part of their body shaved except their head and upper lip. Ten and even twelve have wives common to them, and particularly brothers among brothers, and parents among their children; but if there be any issue by these wives, they are reputed to be the children of those by whom respectively each was first espoused when a virgin.

Chapter 15

The horse and charioteers of the enemy contended vigorously in a skirmish with our cavalry on the march; yet so that our men were conquerors in all parts and drove them to their woods and hills; but, having slain a great many, they pursued too eagerly, and lost some of their men. But the enemy, after some time had elapsed, when our men were off their guard, and occupied in the fortification of the camp, rushed out of the woods, and making an attack upon those who were placed on duty before the camp, fought in a determined manner; and two cohorts being sent by Caesar to their relief, and these severally the first of two legions, when these had taken up their position at a very small distance from each other, as our men were disconcerted by the unusual mode of battle, the enemy broke through the middle of them most courageously, and retreated thence in safety. That day, Q. Laberius Durus, a tribune of the soldiers, was slain. The enemy, since more cohorts were sent against them, were repulsed.

Chapter 16

In the whole of this method of fighting since the engagement took place under the eyes of all and before the camp, it was perceived that our men, on account of the weight of their arms, inasmuch as they could neither pursue [the enemy when] retreating, nor dare quit their standards, were little suited to this kind of enemy; that the horse also fought with great danger, because they [the Britons] generally retreated even designedly, and, when they had drawn off our men a short distance from the legions, leaped from their chariots and fought on foot in unequal [and to them advantageous] battle. But the system of cavalry engagement is wont to produce equal danger, and indeed the same, both to those who retreat and to those who pursue. To this was added, that they never fought in close order, but in small parties and at great distances, and had detachments placed [in different parts], and then the one relieved the other, and the vigorous and fresh succeeded the wearied.

Chapter 17

The following day the enemy halted on the hills, a distance from our camp, and presented themselves in small parties, and began to challenge our horse to battle with less spirit than the day before. But at noon, when Caesar had sent three legions, and all the cavalry, with C. Trebonius, the lieutenant, for the purpose of foraging, they flew upon the foragers suddenly from all quarters, so that they did not keep off [even] from the standards and the legions. Our men making an attack on them vigorously, repulsed them; nor did they cease to pursue them until the horse, relying on relief, as they saw the legions behind them, drove the enemy precipitately before them, and slaying a great number of them, did not give them the opportunity either of rallying, or halting, or leaping from their chariots. Immediately after this retreat, the auxiliaries who had assembled from all sides, departed; nor after that time did the enemy ever engage with us in very large numbers.

Chapter 18

Caesar, discovering their design, leads his army into the territories of Cassivellaunus to the river Thames; which river can be forded in one place only and that with difficulty. When he had arrived there, he perceives that numerous forces of the enemy were marshalled on the other bank of the river; the bank also was defended by sharp stakes fixed in front, and stakes of the same kind fixed under the water were covered by the river. These things being discovered from [some] prisoners and deserters, Caesar, sending forward the cavalry, ordered the legions to follow them immediately. But the soldiers advanced with such speed and such ardour, though they stood above the water by their heads only, that the enemy could not sustain the attack of the legions and of the horse, and quitted the banks, and committed themselves to flight.

Chapter 19

Cassivellaunus, as we have stated above, all hope [rising out] of battle being laid aside, the greater part of his forces being dismissed, and about 4,000 charioteers only being left, used to observe our marches and retire a little from the road, and conceal himself in intricate and woody places, and in those neighbourhoods in which he had discovered we were about to march, he used to drive the cattle and the inhabitants from the fields into the woods; and, when our cavalry, for the sake of plundering and ravaging the more freely, scattered themselves among the fields, he used to send out charioteers from the woods by all the well-known roads and paths, and to the great danger of our horse, engage with them; and this source of fear hindered them from straggling very extensively. The result was, that Caesar did not allow excursions to be made to a great distance from the main body of the legions and ordered that damage should be done to the enemy in ravaging their lands, and kindling fires only so far as the legionary soldiers could, by their own exertion and marching, accomplish it.

Chapter 20

In the meantime, the Trinobantes, almost the most powerful state of those parts, from which the young man, Mandubratius, embracing the protection of Caesar, had come to the continent of Gaul to [meet] him (whose father, Imanuentius, had possessed the sovereignty in that state, and had been killed by Cassivellaunus; he himself had escaped death by flight), send ambassadors to Caesar, and promise that they will surrender themselves to him and perform his commands; they entreat him to protect Mandubratius from the violence of Cassivellaunus, and send to their state someone to preside over it, and possess the government. Caesar demands forty hostages from them, and corn for his army, and sends Mandubratius to them. They speedily performed the things demanded, and sent hostages to the number appointed, and the corn.

Chapter 21

The Trinobantes being protected and secured from any violence of the soldiers, the Cenimagni, the Segontiaci, the Ancalites, the Bibroci, and the Cassi, sending emissaries, surrendered themselves to Caesar. From them he learns that the capital town of Cassivellaunus was not far from that place, and was defended by woods and morasses, and a very large number of men and of cattle had been collected in it. (Now the Britons, when they have fortified the intricate woods, in which they are wont to assemble for the purpose of avoiding the incursion of an enemy, with an intrenchment and a rampart, call them a town.) Thither he proceeds with his legions: he finds the place admirably fortified by nature and art; he, however, undertakes to attack it in two directions. The enemy, having remained only a short time, did not sustain the attack of our soldiers, and hurried away on the other side of the town. A great amount of cattle was found there, and many of the enemy were taken and slain in their flight.

Chapter 22

While these things are going forward in those places, Cassivellaunus sends messengers into Kent, which, we have observed above, is on the sea, over which districts four several kings reigned, Cingetorix, Carvilius, Taximagulus and Segonax, and commands them to collect all their forces, and unexpectedly assail and storm the naval camp. When they had come to the camp, our men, after making a sally, slaying many of their men, and also capturing a distinguished leader named Lugotorix, brought back their own men in safety. Cassivellaunus, when this battle was reported to him as so many losses had been sustained, and his territories laid waste, being alarmed most of all by the desertion of the states, sends ambassadors to Caesar [to treat] about a surrender through the mediation of Commius the Atrebatian. Caesar, since he had determined to pass the winter on the continent, on account of the sudden revolts of Gaul, and as much of the summer did not remain, and he perceived that even that could be easily protracted, demands hostages, and prescribes what tribute Britain should pay each year to the Roman people; he forbids and commands Cassivellaunus that he wage not war against Mandubratius or the Trinobantes.

Chapter 23

When he had received the hostages, he leads back the army to the sea, and finds the ships repaired. After launching these, because he had a large number of prisoners, and some of the ships had been lost in the storm, he determines to convey back his army at two embarkations. And it so happened, that out of so large a number of ships, in so many voyages, neither in this nor in the previous year was any ship missing which conveyed soldiers; but very few out of those which were sent back to him from the continent empty, as the soldiers of the former convoy had been disembarked, and out of those (sixty in number) which Labienus had taken care to have built, reached their destination; almost all the rest were driven back, and when Caesar had waited for them for some time in vain, lest he should be debarred from a voyage by the season of the year, inasmuch as the equinox was at hand, he of necessity stowed his soldiers the more closely, and, a very great calm coming on, after he had weighed anchor at the beginning of the second watch, he reached land at break of day and brought in all the ships in safety.

Endnotes

Foreword

1. F.W. Hardman, LL.D., F.S.A., and W.P.D. Stebbing, F.S.A., F.G.S, 'Stonar and the Wantsum Channel', *Archaeologia Cantiana* – Vol. 53, 1940, p.71.
2. T. Rice Holmes, *Ancient Britain and the Invasions of Julius Caesar* (Clarendon Press, Oxford, 1909), p.519.
3. A.M. Sellar, *Bede's Ecclesiastical History of England* (Christian Classics Ethereal Library), Chapter XXV.
4. Birgitta Hoffmann, *The Roman Invasion of Britain, Archaeology versus History* (Pen & Sword, Barnsley, 2013), pp.22-3.
5. See: roman-britain.co.uk/military/camps england.

Introduction

1. Salway, *Roman Britain*, footnote p.33.
2. Julius Caesar, *The Gallic Wars*, Book IV paras 20 to 38 and Book V paras 1 to 23.
3. Rice Holmes, *Ancient Britain and the Invasions of Julius Caesar*, pp.517-737.

Chapter 1: Caesar's Own Account

1. This chapter is a condensed version of Caesar's own account – see note 2 above.
2. Caesar *The Gallic Wars* Book V para 1.
3. ibid, para 16.

Chapter 2: Rome in the First Century BC

1. Beard *SPQR* p.93.
2. ibid, p.94.

Chapter 3: Caesar the Man

1. Isenberg. *Caesar*, p.24.
2. Boswell, *The Life of Samuel Johnson*, p.24.
3. Meier, *Caesar*, p.213.
4. ibid, p.224.
5. ibid, p.287.
6. ibid, p.304.
7. ibid, p.423.
8. Irwin, *Caesar*, p.140.

Chapter 4: The Roman Army in the First Century BC

1. Goldsworthy, *The Complete Roman Army*, p.7.
2. ibid.
3. ibid, p.49.
4. Vegetius, cited in Peddie, *The Roman War Machine*, p.19.
5. ibid, p.39.
6. ibid, p.89.
7. ibid, p.48.
8. Goldsworthy, p.178.
9. Peddie, p.25.
10. ibid, p.122.
11. ibid, p.57.

Chapter 5: The Invasion of Gaul

1. Meier, p.273.
2. ibid, p.280.
3. Goldsworthy, p.166.

Chapter 6: Britain at the Time of the Invasion

1. Berresford Ellis, *Caesar's Invasion of Britain*, p.58.
2. Salway, p.14.

3. Berresford Ellis, p.18.
4. ibid, p.58.
5. *The collected poems of G K Chesterton* (1927).
6. Berresford Ellis, p.27.
7. ibid, p.30.
8. ibid, p.44.

Chapter 7: The Invasion of 55 BC

1. Rice Holmes *Ancient Britain and the Invasions of Julius Caesar*, pp.565-85.
2. ibid, p.584.
3. The estimate of 50,000 men is most probably low. It is difficult to estimate the total number but given the fact that the legionaries and cavalry alone would have totalled approximately 44,000, if you add to that, the auxiliaries, slaves, traders, hostages and other camp followers, it can immediately be seen that the total would have been significantly in excess of 50,000.
4. Rice Holmes, p.585. At the end of twenty pages of reasoning, Rice Holmes states emphatically that Wissant was not Portus Itius.
5. Rice Holmes, p.586.
6. Caesar *The Gallic Wars*, Book IV para 20. Some translations have this as 'lies towards the North'.
7. Various sources searched via the internet.
8. Bishop, *Folkestone*, p.10.
9. *Archaeologia Cantiana*, Volume 3, 1860, pp.1-18.
10. ibid, p.8.
11. ibid, Volume 1, 1858, p.95.
12. Despite a thorough search, I have been unable to find any reference to the Malms other than in nineteenth century writings on the invasions of Julius Caesar, nor any evidence physically. This is not to say that they do not exist.

Chapter 8: The Invasion of 54 BC

1. Caesar, *The Gallic Wars*, Book V para 18.
2. Rice Holmes, p.697. He writes 'The claims of Brentford have, however, recently been advocated by Mr Montagu Sharpe in a

pamphlet which contains some real evidence. From information supplied by Messrs W. S. Bunting and W. Benell of the Thames Conservancy, and by Conservancy Inspector G. J. Rough, he shows that a line of stakes, of which some still remain "for about 400 yards below Isleworth Ferry", extended thirty years ago for about a mile up the river from "Old England" opposite the mouth of the Brent and that no other ancient stakes have been discovered in the lower river during dredging operations.' The stakes could, of course, have been placed there for any number of reasons.

3. Rufus Noel-Buxton was the son of a Minister in Ramsay Macdonald's Government who had been raised to the peerage. He was convinced that the Romans had forded the river at Westminster and that there was a ford there during the middle ages. He estimated that the depth would be 5ft at low tide and as he was 6ft 3in he was convinced he could walk across. Crowds of people came out to see him very nearly succeed. He later walked across the Severn and the Humber.

4. Wheeler, R.E.M., *London in Roman Times*, London 1930, cited in Thornhill P., A 'Lower Thames Ford and the Campaigns of 54BC and 43AD', in *Archaeologia Cantiana* Volume 92 1976, p.120.

5. Thornhill P., 'A Lower Thames Ford and the Campaigns of 54BC and 43AD' in *Archaeologia Cantiana*, Volume 92 1976, p.119.

6. The internet – principally Wikipedia.

7. Thornhill, Volume 92 1976, p.127.

8. Caesar *The Gallic Wars*, Book V para 9.

9. Caesar *The Gallic Wars*, Book V para 9.

10. *The Gentleman's Magazine*, October 1843, p.398.

11. Ireland, *History of the County of Kent*, p.522. On Chilham, Camden wrote: 'The current tradition among the people here is that Julius Caesar incamped here in his second expedition against the Britans [sic], and that thence it was called *Julham* or *Julius's Station*. And, if I mistake not, they have truth on their side. For Caesar relates that after marching in the night 12 miles he had his first engagement with the Britans on a river and having

driven them into the woods there, he fortified his camp where by felling a number of trees the Britans had a spot excellently fortified by nature and art. Now this place is exactly 12 miles from the shore, nor is there any other river in the way; so that he must necessarily have made his first encampment here. He staid [sic] here 10 days with his army till his fleet which had suffered by a storm was refitted and drawn on shore. Below this town is a tumulus covered with green turf, under which they say was buried many ages since one *Jullaber,* whom some fancy a giant, others a witch. For myself, as I think some antient memorial is concealed under this name, I am almost persuaded that Laberius Durus the military Tribune was buried here, having been slain by the Britans in the march from the fore-mentioned camp, and from him the tumulus was called Jul-laber, (Camden's *Britannia Kent* (Hutchinson 1977)). Chilham is just over 1mile west of Denge Wood by the west bank of the Stour.

12. There has been a tradition that on the second occasion Caesar landed he did so at Deal. Since Deal and Walmer are close by, for those who argue that Walmer was the site of the first landing, this can be regarded as a tradition that he landed at much the same place as he did the year before.

Chapter 9: Analysis of the Conventional View

1. Rice Holmes, p.665.
2. ibid, p.685.
3. ibid, pp.595-665.
4. idid, 665.
5. ibid.
6. ibid, p.696.
7. ibid, p.697.

Chapter 10: The Campaign in Britain – Success or Failure?

1. Caesar *The Gallic Wars*, Book IV para 20.

Chapter 11: Britain after Caesar

1. Bedoyere de la, *Roman Britain, a New History*, p.26.
2. ibid, p.26.
3. Myres, *The English Settlements*, p.203.
4. ibid, p.208.
5. ibid, p.211.

Bibliography

Archaeologia Cantiana. (Kent Archaeological Society 1858 to 2017)

Beard, Mary. *S.P.Q.R. A History of Ancient Rome* (Profile Books, 2016)

Bedoyere de la, Guy. *Roman Britain a New History* (Thames and Hudson, 2013)

Berresford Ellis, Peter. *Caesar's Invasion of Britain* (Constable and Company, 1994)

Bishop, C.H. *Folkestone* (Headley Brothers, 1973)

Boswell, James. *The Life of Samuel Johnson* (J. M. Dent & Sons, 1973)

Camden, William, *Britannia Kent* (Hutchinson edition 1977)

Frere, Sheppard. *Britannia* (Book Club Associates, 1974)

Fuller, J.F.C. *Julius Caesar: Man, Soldier & Tyrant* (Wordsworth Editions, 1998)

Goldsworthy, Adrian. *The Complete Roman Army* (Thames & Hudson, 2011)

Handford, S.A. (revised by Gardner, Jane. F) *Caesar The Conquest Of Gaul* (Penguin Books, 1982)

Holmes, T. Rice. *Ancient Britain and the Invasions of Julius Caesar* (Oxford, 1907)

Ireland, W.H. *History of the County of Kent* (London, 1829)

Isenberg, Irwin. *Caesar* (Cassell. London, 1965)

Mattingly, David. *An Imperial Possession* (Penguin Books, 2007)

Meier, Christian. *Caesar* (HarperCollins, 1995)

Myres, J.N.L. *The English Settlements* (Oxford University Press, 1986)

Peddie, John. *Invasion* (Alan Sutton Publishing, 1987)

Peddie, John. *The Roman War Machine* (Sutton Publishing, 2004)

Salway, Peter. *Roman Britain* (Oxford University Press, 1981)

Smurthwaite, David. *The Complete Guide to the Battlefields of Britain* (Michael Joseph, 1993)

Ward, John. *Roman Britain* (Parkgate Books, 1997)

Index